D1236819

THE
BUSINESS
OF
SPIRITS

THE
BUSINESS
OF
SPIRITS

How Savvy Marketers, Innovative Distillers, and Entrepreneurs Changed How We Drink

NOAH ROTHBAUM

PUBLISHING

New York

This publication is designed to provide accurate and authoritative information in regard to the subject matter covered. It is sold with the understanding that the publisher is not engaged in rendering legal, accounting, or other professional service. If legal advice or other expert assistance is required, the services of a competent professional should be sought.

Vice President and Publisher: Maureen McMahon
Editorial Director: Jennifer Farthing
Acquisitions Editor: Shannon Berning
Development Editor: Joshua Martino
Production Editor: Dominique Polfliet
Production Designer: Todd Bowman
Cover Designer: Rod Hernandez

© 2007 by Noah Rothbaum

Published by Kaplan Publishing, a division of Kaplan, Inc.
1 Liberty Plaza, 24th Floor
New York, NY 10006

Printed in the United States of America

September 2007
10 9 8 7 6 5 4 3 2 1

ISBN-13: 978-1-4277-5475-2

Kaplan Publishing books are available at special quantity discounts to use for sales promotions, employee premiums, or educational purposes. Please email our Special Sales Department to order or for more information at *kaplanpublishing@kaplan.com*, or write to Kaplan Publishing, 1 Liberty Plaza, 24th Floor, New York, NY 10006.

Contents

Introduction: Happy Hour vii

1. The Ghost of Prohibition 1
2. A Singular Sensation 17
3. Vodka Straight Up 39
4. The Cocktail Comeback 63
5. Welcome to the Softer Side of Spirits 95
6. The New, New Thing 129
7. Last Call 159

Acknowledgments 167
References 169
Index 179

INTRODUCTION

Happy Hour

. . . .

ON A BEAUTIFUL evening in September 2006, a giant white party tent perched on a bluff overlooking the Potomac River was the unlikely setting for a historic moment. From a distance, the tent and the afterglow of fireworks could have been mistaken for a fancy Beltway wedding or perhaps a fundraiser to help move a candidate into the Capital's most desired address.

It was neither. Among the assorted Washington movers and shakers, lobbyists and legislators, hacks and spin masters, were a table or two of celebrity guests: bourbon distillers who had come up from Kentucky. These men had a made a special bottling of rye whiskey to honor George Washington, who had owned one of the country's earliest commercial distilleries. And on this balmy night, the first few of these special bottles of rye were to be auctioned off to raise funds for Mount Vernon, Washington's home and a historical site.

The first two bottles, whose contents just a few hours ago had safely been inside a wooden cask, formed a single lot. The very first bottle would stay at Mount Vernon, and the second bottle would go home with the lucky bidder. The organizers of the event, the

Distilled Spirits Council of the United States (DISCUS), were unsure of the opening bid. How much would someone pay for such a bottle? The audience was filled with well-heeled diners as well as heavy hitters from most of the big spirits companies. The bidding started at a reasonable $2,500 and began to rise quickly, soon passing $10,000, then $20,000, then—incredibly—$30,000. When the bidding finished, Marvin Shanken, the publisher of *Wine Spectator* and *Cigar Aficionado* known for his trademark bushy mustache and fat cigars, had paid a staggering $100,000 for the bottle. It was the highest price ever paid for American whiskey and an inconceivable sum for a bottle of humble rye. Some dinner guests had wondered if anyone would pay $2,500 for the bottle.

Welcome to the new era of spirits—when distillers are celebrities, tequila is for sipping, and whisk(e)y sells for vintage Bordeaux wine prices. These days, even something as simple as buying a bottle of vodka can be a major decision. Today, it's not uncommon for shoppers to find dozens of vodkas from all over the world, including Russia, Sweden, Iceland, France, Holland, Scotland, and even San Francisco, not to mention cases of single malt whisky, bourbons, tequilas, gins, and rums in bottles of all shapes and sizes. Just finding your favorite brand can take some hunting. According to Information Resources, a company that tracks supermarket checkout sales, over 6,700 different spirit bottles (SKUs) are on the market. On average, each store stocks nearly 97 different bottles, and some very large or specialty stores stock literally hundreds of bottles from which to choose. New York's Park Avenue Liquor Shop carries over 400 single malts alone.

Store shelves are practically groaning under an ever-increasing load because Americans are again thirsty for hard alcohol. From the mid-1970s through the mid-1990s, spirit consumption was declining as people switched to drinking beer, wine, and soft drinks. But during the last decade, the spirits industry has experienced a renaissance. According to DISCUS, from 1997 to 2005, retail sales of spirits (in stores, bars, and restaurants) have climbed nearly 60 percent, exceeding over $53 billion in 2005 alone. Americans aren't just spending more but are also drinking more spirits. According to a report from The International Wine and Spirit Record, commissioned for the 2007 Vinexpo conference, from 2001 to 2005, per capita consumption of spirits increased by 9 percent and is expected to increase by almost an additional 6 percent by 2010. That's pretty impressive, especially considering that overall per capita alcohol consumption has been decreasing steadily since the 1970s. Spirits are so popular that even beer consumption has been affected. From 2001 to 2006, beer's share of the alcohol market, according to DISCUS, has been steadily decreasing. How bad has it gotten? Anheuser-Busch reported in 2005 that sales were almost flat; as a result, the company is trying to enter the spirits market.

Spirit consumption is up so much, many distilleries are running at full capacity 24 hours a day, 6 or 7 days a week. A number of brands are also expanding the size of their distilleries. Tequila Don Julio shut down in the fall of 2006 to complete a renovation that almost doubled the company's annual production. Diageo is spending almost $200 million to increase its Scottish whisky production. In Kentucky, the demand for rye and bourbon has led Jim Beam to invest $70 million in expanding its distillery and warehouses.

It's not just increased spirit sales that's drawing attention but also what people are drinking. What's now driving the spirits industry isn't plastic gallon bottles of so-called "value" brands. The biggest growth in sales has been in premium or super-premium spirits, like Grey Goose, Patrón, and the Glenlivet. Between 2002 and 2005 alone, according to DISCUS, overall case sales of all premium spirits grew by nearly 19 percent, while over the same period, sales of value spirits just grew by over 2 percent. The trend makes sense, considering that many of the new bottles hitting shelves are high-priced offerings. Ever since Grey Goose displaced Absolut a decade ago and broke the $30 ceiling (Absolut sold for about $15 at the time), there has been a race to produce ever more expensive spirits.

And it's not just pricey vodka. With the number of vodkas seemingly multiplying every day, spirit companies began looking for other spirits categories that could be given luxury makeovers. As a result, tequila has been able to shed its frat-boy image, and now a slew of expensive, aged, 100 percent blue agave sipping tequilas are available. One need look no further than the new Corzo tequila for proof. Corzo sells for about $60 and is packaged in clear, square, flasklike bottles. The undeniable hipness is no accident. The bottle was designed by Fabien Baron, the creative director of *Vogue* (France) and designer of the distinctive cK One perfume bottle and ad campaign. How hot is tequila? Sidney Frank, the founder of Grey Goose, was trying to turn the high-end tequila brand Corazon into another household name before he died at the beginning of 2006. Even white rum, famous for being mixed with Coke, has gotten a face-lift. One example is the new Starr African Rum, which is sold in a distinctive deep red pyramid and is a favorite of celebrities.

Even already pricey single malt whisky has become more deluxe. Not long ago, Macallan produced a $6,000 50-year-old vintage in a special Lalique crystal decanter. (You can forget about buying a bottle—it's sold out.) That's a relative bargain compared to the price of some other vintage whiskies. In March 2005, Glenfiddich auctioned off a bottle of 1937 whisky for $20,000 and a bottle of 60-year-old Macallan was sold to a private collector for a whopping £35,000 (about $70,000). You can blame the recent vintage whisky craze for pushing up prices. In 1996 a bottle of the same 60-year-old Macallan sold for just £12,000 (about $24,000). The increase in value of this bottle of whisky was more than double the growth of the S&P 500 Index during the same period.

The demand makes sense. Over the last 20 years, America's thirst for Scotch whisky, especially expensive single malt, has been unquenchable. The United States is easily the largest export market for the spirit, and according to the Scotch Whisky Association, the American market continues to grow. While the number of bottles imported from Scotland only increased 2 percent from 2004 to 2005, the value of the whisky imported grew by 10 percent. American palates are definitely becoming more discerning. That's in sharp contrast to many markets in Western Europe. In 2005, overall exports to European Union countries were down 11 percent. In some countries, like Spain and Germany, imports were down even further. But the scotch industry is finding a lift from unlikely sources: Asia, up by 24 percent; South America, up 19 percent, and even India, up 89 percent. One reason for the growth in these developing markets is that drinkers are adapting scotch to their local tastes. In China, drinkers have started mixing whisky with green tea.

The growth of the spirits market hasn't gone unnoticed by Wall Street. The increase in sales and profits has led to a series of mergers and acquisitions. Out of what once was largely a group of small or family-run companies, a few giant players have emerged who control most of the industry. As a result, small brands have grown into brand names recognized around the world. The mechanization of distilleries allows companies to keep up with the ever-increasing global demand.

Spirit companies are also getting more exposure on television. After Prohibition ended, the industry decided against TV and radio advertising. Even though the sale of alcohol was legal, the country's attitudes towards drinking were still very conservative. Television was also a relatively new medium, and according to Frank Coleman, senior vice president of DISCUS, most shows aired during the so-called "family hour." The industry thought that the TV ban was socially responsible.

But since 1996, this position has changed. The spirit companies argued that the country was ready for spirit ads and the self-imposed ban put them at a disadvantage, especially since beer companies had used television expertly to promote their products. Plus, with the number of niche channels, a spirit ad could reach a specific targeted adult audience. Hundreds of channels, including dozens of cable stations like CNN, Bravo, and USA Network, have run alcohol ads. Between 2001 and 2005, according to the Center on Alcohol Marketing and Youth (CAMY) at Georgetown University, the alcohol industry collectively spent $4.7 billion for 1.4 million television commercials. In 2005, spirit companies, according to CAMY, spent $122 million on cable TV spots, up from just $5 million in 2001. Over that period, the number of spirit ads increased from 1,973 to 46,854.

The 55-year-old restriction on liquor companies sponsoring NASCAR teams was also lifted before the 2005 race season. Because NASCAR is a family sport, the racing association had decided that spirits advertising wasn't appropriate. Over the years, this ban began to soften. NASCAR already allowed beer and malt liquor companies to sponsor teams, and some tracks even allowed spirit companies to advertise on billboards. Reportedly one of the reasons for the rule change was the drivers' struggle to find sponsors. Liquor companies were more than willing to help. Race officials also argued that spirits have become as morally acceptable as beer to race fans. "We felt the time was right," NASCAR president Mike Helton told the Associated Press. "Attitudes have changed, and spirits companies have a long record of responsible advertising." (NASCAR also requires the sponsoring spirits companies to produce ads promoting responsible drinking.) Spirits giants Diageo, which owns Smirnoff and Johnnie Walker, and Brown-Foreman, which owns Jack Daniel's and Finlandia, have already sponsored racing teams.

States are also loosening rules and regulations to make spirits easier to buy. Even though Prohibition ended almost 75 years ago, the legacy of the temperance movement lives on. In 18 states, including Vermont, Pennsylvania, and Montana, the government controls the sale of spirits at the wholesale or retail level by operating the only licensed liquor stores. In other states, like New York, arcane laws prevent liquor store owners from having more than one location. But laws are slowly changing. You can now buy alcohol on Sunday in 34 states. Twelve of these states have legalized Sunday liquor sales since 2002. In 42 states, it is now legal to host tastings of spirits in liquor stores. It seems hard to believe, but almost a third of these states have only legalized this practice in the last five years. This is significant because the ability to hand out samples allows stores to introduce buyers to new spirits, which is especially helpful for selling premium and super-premium bottles.

Not only have large spirit companies profited from this boom in the popularity of liquor. Microdistilleries have also sprung up across the country. According to Bill Owens, president and founder of the American Distilling Institute, there are now 88 craft distilleries in 27 states, up from 50 just five years ago. That includes a number of microbreweries that make spirits in addition to beers. Even the well-known Dogfish Head brewery now makes several kinds of spirits at its Rehoboth Beach, Delaware, facility. The brewery produces a seasonal selection of flavored vodkas and a variety of rums, including pineapple and banana.

And to drink your premium spirits, you may want more than just a humble tumbler or water glass. Riedel, the Austrian crystal wine glass manufacturer famous for promoting the idea that appreciating each type of wine requires a specific shape of wine glass, has introduced 18 specialized spirit glasses since 1980. There's even one for stone fruit spirits and another for grappa.

One reason for the sudden interest in hard alcohol is the rebirth of the cocktail. Dot-com millionaires looking for pricey drinks in fancy lounges as well as the TV show *Sex and the City* inspired the trend of ordering cosmos and sour apple martinis. Although the show is off the air and the cosmo fad seems a little dated, the popularity of mixed drinks doesn't seem to have abated. If anything, the Jell-O colored cocktails of the late 90s served as an introduction into more traditional mixed drinks. (And when people order their cocktails, they're even specifying by brand name which spirit they want used.)

How big is the phenomenon? *Food & Wine* magazine proclaimed 2006 to be the year of the cocktail. Across the country, bars are adding cocktail menus with pricey drinks. A couple of years ago, a $16 mojito would have sounded ridiculous, but now bars everywhere are devising ever more outlandish and expensive concoctions. (Care for the $10,000 diamond martini at the Blue Bar in New York's Algonquin hotel? The drink is actually served with a diamond.) Bars justify these high prices by using traditional techniques, like muddling, and fresh ingredients, like mint leaves and freshly squeezed lime juice. Some bars even have invested in special ice machines that produce giant cubes, which won't melt quickly and water down your drink. Some nightclubs and lounges ingeniously require people who want to sit at a table to order a few bottles. The clubs usually only serve prestigious premium spirits like Grey Goose or Cristal champagne, which cost hundreds of dollars more than their standard retail price. (At least mixers are usually included.)

Another major factor in the recent success of spirits is that many distillers have changed the taste of their products. Single malts are now routinely aged in different types of casks, which smooth out the spirit and often impart a fruity taste. During the fall of 2006, Glenfiddich even released a Scotch that had been aged in a rum cask. These vintages appeal to both whisky drinkers and nondrinkers alike. This isn't the only initiative to make whisky more appealing. A new company founded by the former master distiller at Macallan is making whisky that is labeled by its taste (smooth, spicy, or smoky) instead of its age or where it was distilled. The company hopes the simpler labels will be more memorable and attract a wider range of drinkers. Another company is even flavoring whiskey with vanilla so that it can be mixed easily with Coke or other mixers.

Along with changing the flavor of spirits, companies are also changing the way they are marketed. Bottle design has in some ways become more important than the spirit that's inside. One of the lessons the industry learned from Grey Goose was that consumers are impressed by reverse labels, frosted glass, and distinctive bottle shapes. But Sidney Frank didn't invent this concept. For decades, the eye-catching green glass of the Tanqueray gin bottle made it one of the industry's most recognizable spirits. But when Diageo recently released the premium Tanqueray Ten, the company used an even more exotic green bottle. Shaped like a slim statuette, it is almost devoid of any label except for what looks like a small pennant and wax seal.

Just like wine sellers, spirits marketers realized that consumers like to know a little backstory about the brand, even if it is invented or makes little sense. So spirit advertising doesn't just tout the quality of the alcohol but the virtues of where it is distilled and the history of the brand. For instance, some of the trucks delivering Wild Turkey are now emblazoned with the slogan "not the newest thing but the original thing."

No wonder it can take you a while to pick out a bottle of alcohol! For the last decade, the spirits industry has been booming and evolving. And now, more than 70 years since the end of Prohibition, it's Happy Hour for the industry and drinkers. Over the next seven chapters, these and other trends will be discussed. And to get in the proper reading mood, pour yourself a dram of your favorite whisky or mix up a cocktail. Cheers!

CHAPTER ONE

Courtesy of the '21' Club

The Ghost
of Prohibition

· · · · · · · ·

To GET TO the storeroom of New York's legendary '21' Club, cross the dining room with its constellation of corporate and sports memorabilia, slip through the bustling kitchen, and head down a flight of steep stairs. There, in an unremarkable brick-lined hallway, is a pencil-sized hole. Insert an 18-inch piece of wire into it, and like something out of an Indiana Jones movie, a two-and-a-half-ton hidden door swings open, revealing a fine spirits and wine collection. This hidden storeroom was built during Prohibition and is actually below the adjoining townhouse (19 West 52nd Street). It was constructed so the owners could truthfully say that there wasn't any alcohol on the premises if the restaurant was raided.

But this quaint relic of Prohibition isn't the only legacy of that era, which still haunts the United States. Almost 75 years after Congress overwhelmingly passed the 21st Amendment ending the 13-year period of Prohibition, the U.S. is still trying to figure out how to regulate the sale of alcohol. This is particularly troublesome given the fact that the spirits industry is now booming and sales are increasing every year. From 1997 to 2005, retail sales of spirits (in

stores, bars, and restaurants), according to the Distilled Spirits Council of the United States, have increased nearly 60 percent and topped $53 billion in 2005. And don't expect spirit sales to slow down any time soon. By 2010, per capita consumption of spirits is forecasted to increase by almost another 6 percent. But as store shelves fill up with a dazzling variety of bottles and consumers develop a taste for increasingly expensive spirits, the country is now forced to deal with its relationship with alcohol.

The problem stems from the fact that the 21st Amendment only repealed the 18th Amendment; it didn't spell out exactly how alcohol sales would be controlled. Congress left those decisions up to the individual states. As a result, the United States has an almost incomprehensible patchwork of alcohol-related laws that vary greatly from state to state and sometimes county to county. No two states have exactly the same laws regarding alcohol. For instance, the legal drinking age of 21 only became standard in 1998 after the federal government threatened to withhold funding to states that didn't comply. Even the legal alcohol content of beer varies across the country.

Once Prohibition ended, legislators remained cautious. In many areas, newly enacted laws were quite restrictive. Four states chose to remain temporarily dry. Across the country, local legislatures passed a variety of laws limiting the purchase of alcohol. Many states enacted "blue laws," which prevented alcohol sales on Sunday. In some areas, it became illegal to purchase alcohol on credit or with a check. Other places forbade the purchase of alcohol on national holidays like Election Day. Several states, including New York, Connecticut, and New Jersey, fixed the amount by which stores could mark up the price of liquor by the bottle. States also passed a slew of laws limiting how alcohol could be advertised. Eighteen states went even further, actually taking over the wholesale and sometimes retail sale of alcohol.

According to an article by veteran wine writer Frank J. Prial in the *New York Times,* many of these laws were "religiously motivated. They were meant to keep alive the Prohibition spirit and try to achieve some of the things Prohibition had failed to do." Even after the temperance movement lost popularity and blue laws for other retail industries loosened up, the restrictive laws concerning alcohol remained on the books. One reason, according to Prial, was the strong lobbying power of the liquor retailers. Many of the laws favored liquor store owners, who were opposed to proconsumer changes, like expanding weekend store hours or ending alcohol price controls. Many store owners didn't want to stay open late at night or all weekend. They were also afraid that an open market would create disastrous price wars. The country's experiment in temperance hadn't succeeded in drying out the country or dampening its thirst for alcoholic beverages, but it did succeed in making alcohol more difficult to obtain.

This chapter of American history is far from over. Many states continue to have arcane alcohol laws on their books. For instance, in Delaware, alcohol sales are currently prohibited when polls are open for national or statewide elections. Shoppers in Virginia's state-run liquor stores cannot use a debit card to make purchases. Fortunately, lawmakers continually revise these statutes, and over the last few years, there has been a push to do away with the most restrictive blue laws. One major reason for this movement is that cash-strapped municipalities are continually on the lookout for new streams of tax revenue. Increased alcohol sales mean more tax dollars. Today, almost three out of every four states allow alcohol sales on Sunday—unheard of only a few years ago. The Distilled Spirits Council of the United States, the alcohol manufacturers' industry advocacy group, which has been pushing for these legal reforms, tabulated that New York State alone could increase tax revenue by $26.7 million just by allowing store owners to stay open on Sunday. And laws have also recently loosened regarding in-store spirit tastings. Since 2001,

15 states have made this change. Now 84 percent of states allow stores to hold spirits tastings, which of course helps to increase sales of new or especially expensive bottles.

The debate over how and if liquor should be sold predates Prohibition—its roots lie in colonial times. To understand the current complex alcohol laws, you must look at the relationship that this country has had with alcohol from its founding. Some of the country's earliest residents were distillers, and some of the goods first produced by Americans were spirits. During the 1700s, the New England colonies produced rum from imported molasses, Pennsylvania farmers distilled rye whiskey from locally grown crops, and Kentucky became known for a new corn-based spirit called bourbon. Even a number of the country's founding fathers were distillers. James Madison was a big beer brewer who supported the foundation of a national brewery. At Mount Vernon, George Washington had a commercial whiskey distillery with five working stills. At his Charlottesville, Virginia, home, Thomas Jefferson planted a vineyard and, like many Americans at the time, brewed his own beer.

At the time, alcohol was perceived to have salutary effects on one's health. According to the National Alcoholic Beverage Control Association (NABCA), life insurance companies even had lower premiums for imbibers. But at the same time, residents of the colonies didn't tolerate public drunkenness, making it a punishable offense. And the colonists are credited with the concept of blue laws that limited the sale of and consumption of alcohol. (One theory is the expression "blue law" comes from the fact that the laws were sometimes printed on blue paper.)

Yet already by the late 1700s, a vocal minority believed spirits to be dangerous. One of the movement's advocates was Reverend Lyman Beecher, father of author Harriet Beecher Stowe, who beseeched his congregation to avoid alcohol. The medical

George Washington: The First Distiller

Founding father of America and the country's spirits industry

George Washington is famous for many reasons. But what is not commonly known about him is that at the end of his life, he was a very successful distiller and entrepreneur. A number of the country's founding fathers produced beer, wine, or whiskey, but Washington actually sold his spirit. At Mount Vernon, his 8,000-acre plantation just outside of Washington, D.C., he grew a number of crops, including wheat and rye. (He also had over 300 slaves working his farm.) Mostly he traded the grains or ground them using his water-powered gristmill. To store the grains, Washington built a unique 16-sided barn. Washington exported his flour to markets as distant as England and Portugal.

But Washington's Scottish farm manager, James Anderson, convinced the former president to turn some of his crops into whiskey. In 1797, Washington constructed out of local stone a 2,250-square-foot distillery near his gristmill and cooperage. At its peak, the distillery had five copper stills that produced 11,000 gallons of whiskey. It was one of the country's largest distilleries. In 1799, the whiskey brought in $7,500, a very handsome profit.

And it was a good time to be in the whiskey business because adult Americans on average drank gallons and gallons of alcohol a year. (Spirits were generally served with meals at Mount Vernon.) Domestic liquor was also in high demand because the British had cut off the country's supply of rum and molasses from the Caribbean. As a result, Washington's whiskey was a best seller, and it sold as quickly as he could make it. Unfortunately, the distillery was only in business for a short time. Just three years after Washington's

(continued)

final presidential term, he died 48 hours after the onset of a sudden throat infection, the distillery shut down shortly thereafter.

Until a few years ago, very little was left of the distillery. In 1997, 200 years after its construction, archeologists discovered the site, and a few years later, with a $2.1 million grant from the Distilled Spirits Council of the United States, work began to reconstruct the facility. In September 2006, the handsome wood and stone building was officially dedicated. You can now visit the working distillery, which is also the home of the first museum dedicated to American distilling. It sits just below the reconstructed gristmill on the banks of the Dogue Run Creek.

A number of well-known bourbon distillers were on hand for the dedication, including Wild Turkey's Eddie Russell and Maker's Mark's Bill Samuels, Jr. They were also there to run a small pot still and to hand-bottle a special rye that had been distilled and aged at Mount Vernon. And in an ironic twist, even the British royals, Washington's old nemesis, were on hand to offer congratulations. Prince Andrew the Duke of York accepted a bottle of the Mount Vernon whiskey and praised the work of Washington's Scottish farm manager. Appropriately, after the ribbon was cut, the crowd toasted Washington with whiskey and then splashed the building with the rest of their drinks.

community also began to investigate the supposed beneficial effects of alcohol on the body. In 1785, Continental Army Surgeon General Dr. Benjamin Rush published "An Inquiry into the Effects of Ardent Spirits," which, according to the National Alcohol Beverage Control Association (NABCA), dismissed the commonly held belief that soldiers needed alcohol to keep in shape. The military community was shocked when Dr. Rush recommended that the army stop distributing rum to the troops. It took almost 50 years before the army finally agreed with him.

The temperance movement continued to grow. In 1851, Maine became the first state to ban the production and sale of potable alcohol. Over several years, 12 more states enacted prohibition laws. But this period of temperance didn't last long. One reason, according to NABCA, was that hordes of heavy-drinking immigrants from Ireland and Germany began washing up on the country's shores, bringing with them a long beer- and spirit-making tradition. According to Ohio State University, annual per capita spirit consumption in 1850 was about four gallons and grew to almost five gallons by 1860—a record that hasn't since been matched.

Though temporarily halted by the Civil War, the debate over alcohol continued in 1872 when a prohibitionist candidate unsuccessfully ran for president of the United States. Several major temperance organizations also formed and began campaigning for bars to close. But at the same time, technical and manufacturing advances, like refrigeration and the national railroad system, made possible the large-scale production and widespread distribution of beer. As a result, beer consumption began to increase rapidly and soon exceeded distilled spirits consumption. Soon large and powerful breweries began to dominate the industry and started signing saloons to exclusive contracts to sell their beer on tap.

There was also a boom in the saloon business, and by 1870, there were over a 100,000 saloons in the country—roughly one for every 400 Americans. Competition was fierce, and profit margins were shaved to the minimum. To attract customers and increase revenue, saloon owners branched out into unsavory businesses like gambling and prostitution. The link between the sale of alcohol and crime was now well established and undeniable. The temperance movement began to make more sense to mainstream America.

At the same time, temperance advocates began working on a grassroots level, backing first local and then state candidates who began winning elections. Seven states were dry by 1909, and according to the NABCA, more than half the states had passed some kind of prohibition laws by 1917. With the country at war with Germany, it was easy for temperance advocates to drum up support for a national alcohol ban and stir up hatred for America's brewers because many of them were of German descent. According to The Gilder Lehrman Institute of American History, Milwaukee brewers were called "the worst of all our German enemies," and their beer was nicknamed "Kaiser brew" by the dries. In 1917, Congress passed the Lever Food and Fuel Act that banned the manufacture of spirits made from grain while the country was at war. It was easy to convince people that the country's resources should be used to support the fight against the Germans instead of being used to make alcohol.

Then Congress passed the 18th Amendment banning the "manufacture, sale or transportation of intoxicating liquors." The National Prohibition Act went into effect on January 16, 1920. But Americans weren't the only ones to go dry. Across Europe, many countries, including Norway, England, and Sweden, also passed laws prohibiting or restricting the consumption of alcohol.

Sadly, the end of crime and corruption that the Amendment's supporters promised never came to fruition. Historians and social critics now believe that Prohibition only exacerbated the problems that were plaguing the United States at the turn of the century. Banning alcohol created an opportunity for gangsters to take control of the spirits industry. As a result, bootleggers and rumrunners became quite powerful and wealthy. These illegal profits were funneled into the pockets of police, judges, and politicians across the country, causing widespread corruption. Even though dries had hoped that shutting down the saloons would result in less crime, the Amendment had the opposite effect. Soon the jails and courts were filled with alcohol-related cases, putting a strain on local municipalities. According to an article from the Cato Institute titled "Alcohol Prohibition Was a Failure" by Mark Thornton, there were 4,000 federal convicts before 1914, but because of Prohibition, that number grew to 26,589 by 1932. At the same time, the number of homicides in big cities, which had been in decline for decades, also increased by 78 percent during Prohibition.

On the most basic level, Prohibition failed because per capita consumption of alcohol did not significantly decrease. People were making their own "bathtub gin" and moonshine as well as drinking in many illegal bars that popped up. In New York City, there were over 30,000 bars, more than twice as many as before the city went dry. But not only New Yorkers were breaking the law. In Cleveland, Ohio, according to the Gilder Lehrman Institute, there were 1,200 bars in 1919, but during Prohibition, more than twice as many illegal bars were open. Worse, according to Thornton, Prohibition also led people to drink spirits with higher alcoholic content because it was easier to transport and conceal these higher-octane drinks. And some drinkers who couldn't obtain alcohol switched to drugs. Prohibition was intended to make people healthier, but the number of Americans dying from alcohol-related causes, according to Thornton, actually increased. The main reason was that the underground alcohol industry was unregulated and some of the spirits it produced were deadly to consume.

By the end of the 1920s, the public's patience and enthusiasm for Prohibition was waning. The corruption and violence had reached new highs. According to NABCA, in Chicago alone, there were over 400 mob killings a year. The bloody Valentine's Day Massacre of 1929 symbolized just how out of control the country had become.

Prohibition might have been tolerated during the Roaring Twenties, but after the Great Depression began on Tuesday, October 29, 1929, it seemed unwise to shut down a viable industry. Not only could the economy use all the alcohol-related jobs, but the government had lost tax revenue on all the illicit alcohol being sold. In 1933, with a newly elected Franklin Delano Roosevelt in the White House, the supposed "Noble Experiment" finally ended.

But lawmakers were given a hard task. There needed to be a way to sell alcohol without causing the pre-Prohibition problems of the distillers and brewers dominating the industry. Each state created a three-tier system to handle the importation, distribution, and sale of spirits, breaking up these three processes to make sure that the distillers and brewers couldn't get too powerful. The way the system usually works is that one company produces or imports the spirits and another distributes them to independently run retail stores or chains. Spirit producers cannot sell directly to consumers or stores. And unlike before Prohibition, distillers can't sign up bars to serve only their products. The three-tier system is supposed to encourage competition. All three types of businesses are also licensed by the government, so that the industry can be closely monitored and held responsible for any abuses. (Licensing also ensures that the appropriate amount of taxes are collected and remitted to the government.)

Over the last few years, however, not only has there been a major consolidation among spirit makers but also among distributors. For many years, spirit distribution was handled by small, local companies. Now in most states, just a couple of huge distributors handle all of the brands. The largest of the large is Southern Wine and Spirits of America, which expected to have sales of over $7 billion in 2006, equal to about a fifth of the total wine and spirits wholesale business. Southern started in Florida in 1968 and, over the last four decades, has evolved into a giant, distributing 5,000 brands in 27 states. Being so large has many advantages, including the fact that a distributor can help push a brand around the country through promotions and marketing. Southern even employs mixologists and sommeliers who can help train restaurant and liquor store staffs.

But a major hurdle for a new spirit is finding a distributor who is willing to carry the brand and actively sell it to store owners. "It's real tough for the little guy to get into the warehouse and out of the warehouse," says Tito Beveridge, founder of Texas-based Tito's Handmade Vodka. The 21st Amendment made it "legal to make it. That doesn't mean you can sell it," he says. Clearly, the three-tier system benefits large brands because a distributor can easily sell thousands of cases without much work. For the most popular brands, the question is not if a store will buy a case but how many cases, while smaller brands often require hand selling to every liquor store owner and restaurant spirits buyer.

In the 18 "control states," the three-tier system is slightly different. In these states, the government assumed control of the wholesaling of alcohol and sometimes also retail sales by creating state-run liquor stores. These control systems were a compromise; alcohol is available, but it isn't promoted so as to keep consumption down. (In fact, in some of these state-run stores, employees are not permitted to offer consumers recommendations.) According to NABCA, the policies are successful: in control states, per capita consumption of spirits is 15.8 percent less than consumption in licensed states. But at the same time, by cutting out private wholesalers and retailers, these states generate almost 100 percent more revenue per gallon than regulated states.

As sprit consumption continues to increase, the laws regarding alcohol sales and distribution will also need to evolve. The United States has some of the most complex alcohol laws in the world, so complex that the European Union has even asked the U.S. government to streamline them. The courts are already on the case. In the spring of 2005, the Supreme Court ruled that wineries could sell and ship wine directly to consumers across the county. The individual states can now choose either to allow these shipments or ban all direct winery sales. In light of this landmark ruling, the idea of

This Beer's for You?

Spirits sales are up, but that's not necessarily good news for beer brewers.

Beer bills itself as America's drink of choice. There's plenty of evidence to support that claim, including the fact that some of the country's founding fathers were very fond of the beverage, not to mention the link between beer and America's other pastime, baseball. But over the last few years, thanks to the popularity of spirits and wine, beer's market share of the overall alcohol industry has been gradually decreasing. It still accounts for more than 50 percent of the market, but that might change over the next few years. According to a report from The International Wine and Spirit Record, commissioned for the 2007 Vinexpo conference, between 2001 and 2005, per capita consumption of beer decreased by over 3 percent and is expected to decrease by an additional 6 percent by 2010.

But the news isn't all bad for brewers. Just as with spirits, sales of higher-end imported and craft beers are up. From 2003 to 2006, according to the Brewers Association, sales of craft beer increased by almost 30 percent. Even though the microbrew craze has cooled off a bit, many of these small breweries have developed a loyal and sometimes national following. Just as with spirits, wine, or coffee, over the last few years, many people have become beer connoisseurs, willing to pay a premium for a better, more complex brew. Around the country, many brewpubs and bars now serve dozens of beers from around the world. Some of these establishments, like The Map Room in Chicago, Illinois, even offer beer classes to teach patrons about what they're drinking. On websites like *Beeradvocate.com*, people vigorously debate the best beers and the top places to enjoy a pint. As a result, sales of craft and imported beers will most likely continue to increase over the next few years.

The big breweries are also working hard to increase sales and change the lowbrow connotation of mass-produced beer. For example, Anheuser-Busch launched the "Here's to Beer" ad campaign in February 2006, which according to the company, "aims to elevate the image of beer." So in addition to the standard message of how friends can bond over a six-pack, the campaign also tried to get drinkers to pair beer with different foods. The campaign's website featured cheese pairing suggestions, beer cocktail recipes, and even food recipes from celebrity chef Todd English that called for beer as an ingredient. To compete with the microbrews, the beer giant has also created a number of limited edition beers that are sold seasonally.

As a backup plan, Anheuser-Busch has created a new division, called Long Tail Libations, to develop spirits. The company's first product, Jekyll & Hyde, is a liqueur made from two spirits that a consumer combines when he's ready to drink it. According to the Associated Press, the president of the company, August Busch IV, disclosed these intentions at the National Conference of State Liquor Administrators in June of 2006. "The loss of beer volume to wine and hard liquor has accelerated in recent years," says Busch. "And if this trend continues, we at Anheuser-Busch will have to re-evaluate our business model going forward in terms of expanding beyond beer and broadening our position within the total alcohol industry."

direct sales of American-made spirits doesn't seem out of the question anymore. Big retailers like Wal-Mart are also pushing for the reform of alcohol laws; Wal-Mart's negotiations with spirit manufacturers are hampered by the structure of the three-tier system. But for consumers and even people involved in the industry, the regulations and restrictions can still be quite confusing. Even though Prohibition is an almost-forgotten era of American history, the effects of the temperance movement will be felt for decades.

CHAPTER TWO

Courtesy of the Author

A Singular
Sensation

· · · · · · · ·

NOT LONG AGO, finding a bottle of Scottish single malt whisky was nearly impossible. Now it's hard to walk into a bar or a liquor store without finding at least one of the three Glens—Glenfiddich, Glenlivet, or Glenmorangie—not to mention the dozens of other single malts that have flooded the U.S. market over the last 20 years. Glenfiddich, which takes credit for creating the category, was first imported to the states in 1963. Before then, almost all of the single malt produced wasn't bottled but was used in whisky blends. Most Americans got their first taste of single malt when it became widely available in the late 1970s or 1980s and ever since have developed an unquenchable taste for it. In fact, during the last few years, the United States has again become the number one market by value for the Scottish whisky industry, a title held by Spain as recently as 2001. In 2005, about 120 million bottles of Scotch whisky, worth about $720 million, were exported to America.

But Scotch is not just thriving in the United States. According to the Scotch Whisky Association, in 2005 overall exports totaled about $4.6 billion—the third highest total on record for the industry.

Sales are booming in Asia, Latin America, and even India. But the largest market by volume for whisky is just across the English Channel in France, where it has become the drink of choice. It's particularly ironic given the country's own noble history of distillation and wine making. And Scotch is only getting more popular; from 2004 to 2005, exports to France increased by 12 percent, for a total of 153.5 million bottles.

Yet most Scottish whisky isn't single malt. In fact, over 90 percent of whisky produced goes into blended whiskies, a mix of a number of single malts and aged grain whisky. For decades, blended whisky has been imported to America and has sold very well. But that's changing as single malt becomes increasingly popular and draws new, younger drinkers. According to experts, for the most part, drinkers of blended whisky are older and more loyal to a single brand that they've been enjoying for years. According to Distilled Spirits Council of the United States (DISCUS), the number of nine-liter cases of single malt sold in the United States increased by over 19 percent between 2002 to 2005. Over the same period, sales of cases of blends only increased by about 3 percent. Most master blenders, however, are quick to point out that these figures are impressive but relative to the overwhelming size of the blended category. And the blenders will even admit that they are quite happy about the attention and the customers that single malt has brought to the industry. "It's great to have a buzz on whisky," says Colin Scott, the master blender at Chivas Regal.

Another reason distillers are happy is that Americans aren't just drinking more Scottish whisky—they're also drinking more expensive whisky. According to the Scotch Whiskey Association, from 2004 to 2005, overall consumption grew by just a few percentage points, but the value of the whisky consumed grew by 10 percent. People are trading up from blends, or even so-called white spirits like vodka and gin, to ever more expensive single malts and,

Monument to Malt: Park Avenue Liquor Shop

Thanks to the popularity boom of single malt whiskies, American drinkers have a huge selection from which to choose. But tracking down bottles from some of the smaller distilleries or buying a limited edition bottling can be challenging. Most liquor stores only stock the most popular brands and the youngest (least expensive) offerings. But one place that is sure to stock even the rarest of whiskies is New York City's Park Avenue Liquor Shop. A virtual nirvana for whisky fans, Park Avenue stocks over 400 single malts alone, not to mention blends, bourbon, cognac, and armagnac. Most of these precious bottles are on display on a huge set of shelves behind the store's registers. People from all over the world come to the shop to pay homage to the collection of whisky and pick up some rare malts.

Park Avenue Liquor Shop, which is actually located on Madison Avenue, began specializing in the expanding single malt whisky category 14 years ago. The whisky section soon began gobbling up shelf space, even forcing the store to jettison some blended whisky and vodkas. "We try to carry as many different distilleries as possible," says the store's vice president, Jonathan Goldstein. "We really became a store that specialized in rare and hard-to-get spirits." In fact, in addition to carrying all the standard fare, Park Avenue now buys whole casks from distillers and does their own limited edition private bottling. In the past, the store has done bottlings with Highland Park, Auchentoshan, and Compass Box. After Goldstein tastes, samples, and finds the perfect cask, it can be on the store's shelves in just three months.

In Scotland, private bottlings are relatively common, and over the last few years, a number of high-end American liquor stores

(continued)

have also begun to offer them. Park Avenue was one of the first to start this trend. Goldstein is always on the lookout for deals with distilleries and is currently selecting casks for the store's next unique offering. The store has branched out, also bottling a bourbon and a rum, and Goldstein is working on doing an exclusive tequila. But even with his loyal and knowledgeable customer base, he admits, "There's no way I can hand sell a certain distillery that's just not very popular here in the States. You have to have a good story behind it for me to consider buying an entire cask."

to a lesser extent, expensive blended whiskies. This is a huge role reversal and coup for the category, which had been steadily losing drinkers to vodka and gin over the last 30 years. Part of the reason for the increase in sales is that single malt whisky has now come to embody the epitome of luxury and wealth, a position that pricey blends like Johnnie Walker and Chivas Regal held in the 1950s and 1960s, or cognac, which was the epitome of sophistication during the 19th century.

Just as upscale bars have to offer jazz and comfy brown leather club chairs, a top shelf full of old single malts is now also a prerequisite. Bar owners are more than happy to stock and serve these malts because they can charge $10 or more for a dram and find them less labor-intensive to serve than cocktails. (New York's Brandy Library perhaps is the extreme, offering 270 different single malts as well as 130 cognacs.)

Around the world, the spirit has become the drink of choice for the well-to-do. During the American tech boom of the late 1990s, sales of expensive single malts took off as people wanted ever rarer and pricier drinks. At the same time, some of the rarest bottles were sent to

Japan, where Scotch became a favorite of Tokyo businessmen. (Soon after, however, the Japanese market for whisky softened as drinkers switched to ordering white spirits and expensive imported wine.) In Asian countries with booming economies, whisky sales have grown greatly. Exports to South Korea, Taiwan, and Thailand increased by at least 24 percent from 2004 to 2005. In Venezuela, scotch sales have skyrocketed. As the price of Venezuelan oil has climbed higher and higher, so too has the demand for whisky. According to a story in the *New York Times,* heavyweight Diageo, owner of dozens of whisky brands including Talisker, Lagavulin, and Dalwhinnie, saw sales in Venezuela increase by a whopping 60 percent in 2005. The increase is especially impressive given the country's own well-respected rum industry and because Venezuela's leftist president Hugo Chavez has attacked the importation of foreign whisky.

However, the demand for single malt is actually a relatively new phenomenon, even though Scotland has been making whisky for hundreds of years. The first written mention of the spirit is an entry into the records of the Scottish Exchequer in 1494. It is likely that the art of distilling so called aqua vitae (water of life) was brought to Scotland by Irish monks even earlier. In the mid-1600s, the highlands of Scotland became the epicenter of whisky production because the land offered plentiful supplies of barley and pure spring water. And perhaps most important, the forbidding terrain also afforded the distillers the perfect hideout from the British Crown's tax collectors, who had imposed punitive taxes on the budding whisky industry in 1644.

These duties didn't stop the highlanders from continuing to distill and perfect their product. By the early 1800s, the taxes were finally lowered, and the whisky trade became legal and regulated. George Smith, founder of the now ubiquitous The Glenlivet, applied for and received the first distilling license in 1824. The company claims he did so at the risk of his life because the other illegal distillers, who were making a good living, were less than happy with his decision to go legit and pay taxes. At the time whisky was generally sold by the barrel to bars around Scotland and Ireland. Some even made it to America.

By 1850, the whisky trade was well established, and companies soon began buying single malt from distilleries and blending it with aged grain whisky. This offered several advantages. The blending mellowed the whisky—grain whisky is a lot lighter than single malt—and made the finished spirit much easier to drink. For example, Johnnie Walker Black Label is 60 percent to 70 percent grain whisky. Red Label's percentage is even greater. Adding grain whisky also allowed blenders to stretch the single malt. Grain whisky wasn't made on the traditional, expensive swan-necked copper stills but on the new, high-volume, more efficient continuous patent stills, also known as Coffey Stills in honor of their inventor, Aeneas Coffey. (These stills are more like the ones used to distill vodka.) When introduced in 1831, the patent still was quite an innovation, and grain whisky continues to be made on it today. Grain whisky doesn't have to be made from malted barley (barley that has been germinated) and was often made from the cheapest grain available, usually unmalted barley, wheat, or corn. Like single malt, it must be aged.

Sales of blends were helped by the widespread marketing campaigns waged by whisky companies. The industry also got a break at the end of the 19th century, thanks to the phylloxera virus. For years, as the small aphid ate its way across European vineyards, no cognac, sherry, or port was produced. The crisis didn't end until the European farmers grafted their vines onto a Texas rootstock that was resistant to the virus. Even though the phylloxera epidemic ended, it gave a big boost to whisky companies and an almost fatal blow to cognac, sherry, and port producers. Drinkers around the world had discovered whisky, which became increasingly popular while sales of cognac never regained the same level of popularity.

The whisky blenders became so successful that they began buying up single malt distilleries, ensuring a continuous supply of quality whisky for their blends. Today, the largest blenders still own many of the single malt distillers. Diageo alone owns 27 different single malt distilleries (about a third of the entire industry) and 2 grain distilleries. (To keep up with demand, in the winter of 2007, the company announced that it was investing almost $200 million to expand whisky production. The plan included the construction of a new malt distillery in Speyside.) The whisky from these distilleries goes into the company's 14 blends, including Johnnie Walker, Bell's, and J&B. A blended whisky brand can be made from dozens of different single malts. For instance, the recipes for J&B and for the 12-year-old Johnnie Walker Black Label each call for a different blend of about 40 malts and grain whiskies.

But just as whisky was truly about to dominate, the industry faced a number of serious problems. Production was first stopped for World War I and then hindered by the global temperance movement, which affected key markets, including, of course, the United States. Soon after Prohibition was repealed, World War II began and production ceased again. As the war was ending in 1944, Winston Churchill decided that the whisky industry should start up again and get a ration of barley. He was afraid that once the war was over, there wouldn't be an adequate supply of whisky for export and it would take years for the distillers to get going again, causing a major blow to the country's peacetime economy.

As the United Kingdom tried to recover from the war during the next decade, the government limited the amount of whisky that could be produced. (It wasn't just the whisky industry that was affected. Certain foods continued to be rationed until the early 1950s.) Fortunately, the restrictions were soon relaxed. Because of the two World Wars and Britain's connection to her former colonies, whisky had been introduced all over the world. Throughout the 1950s and 1960s, blended whisky exports to America grew and, according to DISCUS, reached a peak in 1975 of almost 24 million nine-liter cases.

The good times were short-lived: the economic crises of the late 1970s and early 1980s crippled the whisky industry. Many distilleries were forced to close, many never reopening. According to a story in the whisky enthusiast magazine, *Malt Advocate,* 16 distilleries closed during the first half of the 1980s, and the distilleries that remained open reduced their output. As a result, according to John Hansell, the publisher and editor of *Malt Advocate,* the supply of 20-year-old malt is now running low, while whisky companies have good stock of 30-year-olds from the 1970s. Distillers have responded by increasing prices for 18- or 20-year-old whiskies. To keep products on shelves, some brands are bottling older whisky but putting a younger age on the bottle. (Technically, this truth stretching is permissible, as the age on the label is really only a minimum—but this is clearly not a long-term solution.) Other distilleries are introducing nonvintage whiskies, like Macallan's Cask Strength, which bears no age on the label at all. "They just can't spare the older stuff," says Jonathan Goldstein, vice president of New York's Park Avenue Liquor Shop.

Even though historically, almost all of the single malt went into blends, in the highlands of Scotland and Northern England, there had always been demand for the straight malt. It's no wonder, considering that the whisky has a full-bodied and very rich taste. The range of flavors also runs the gamut from fruity to smoky since each distillery produces a unique tasting whisky.

But even in the home market, it took drinkers many years to begin to appreciate the taste of single malt. One reason was that it just wasn't easy to get your hands on a bottle. Buying single malt in Scotland meant buying from the distillery itself or an independent bottler. Just like a blender, an independent bottler buys new spirit from a distillery and then ages and bottles the whisky. Usually, the whisky bottle bears a label listing both the bottler as well as the distillery where the spirit was produced. "The distillers were happy to sell casks to anyone," says Hansell, because it meant some extra cash.

One of the most famous independent bottlers is Gordon & MacPhail. The company began in 1895 in the town of Elgin, which is very close to the Speyside distillers, and is still in business today. In addition to selling groceries and wine and blending its own whiskies, the company also bottled single malt that it bought from the distillers. Eventually Gordon & MacPhail dropped the groceries to specialize in whisky and wine. Today the company offers 450 of its own bottlings, which range in age from 5 to 60 years, and has a stock of over 700 whiskies. Some of the older whiskies in the company's inventory are extremely rare because they are perhaps the only casks that the distillers didn't sell to blenders.

According to Hansell, the independent bottlers were instrumental in turning people on to single malt scotch. But today, some whisky experts predict the demise of independent bottlers. Because the distillers now bottle their own single malts, they don't want to sell casks and are making it harder for the bottlers to get the whisky. It's more profitable for the distillery to bottle the single malt itself. Also, the master distiller can control the product and determine when a cask should be bottled. Distillers were concerned that the independent bottlers might put out substandard whiskies, which would reflect poorly on the distillery. They also didn't want to compete against themselves by allowing consumers the luxury of choosing between a distiller's product line and the rarer odd cask that had been sold to a private bottler.

After the economic crunch of the late 1970s and early 1980s, the industry was at a crossroads. There were fewer distilleries, but at the same time, American demand for blends was decreasing. According to DISCUS, the volume of Scotch whisky sold in America dropped by almost 44 percent during the '80s. A big reason for this decline was the vodka craze started by a new Swedish brand, Absolut. Unlike whisky, which boasted a long and rich history, Michel Roux's now legendary ad campaign for Absolut used well-known and edgy artists like Andy Warhol and Jean-Michel Basquiat to emphasize the vibrancy and hipness of vodka.

Ironically, while consumers may not have wanted to buy whisky, advances in technology made the spirit much easier and less labor intensive to make. In most distilleries by the 1980s, electric coils replaced the coal fires that historically had heated the stills. It allowed the still workers to regulate the amount of heat easily and keep the stills at a constant temperature without getting up from their seats. The coils were also a lot safer than continually burning coal; distillery fires were not uncommon during the era of coal furnaces. Another time saver dating from the 1960s was the establishment of specialty malters. These malters can prepare the barley to a distiller's exact specifications, down to the amount of moisture in the grain. (Diageo even owns four malters to ensure that its distilleries have a constant and consistent supply.) Now only a handful of distilleries, including Highland Park and Balvenie, still use traditional floor malting.

Whisky companies also began using computers to track each of their casks. According to Douglas McLean Murray, master of whisky at Johnnie Walker, the brand began adding bar codes to casks in 1985. The technology was a great help, given that it has about 8 million casks aging in different warehouses. Now when Murray puts together a Johnnie Walker blend, a computer generates a list of the casks to pull. Because the computer tracks all the blends being made, the warehouse workers can make fewer trips and get casks from the same warehouse for several different whiskies at the same time. Thanks to these advances, output increased, and the number of workers employed by the distilleries dropped. It used to take a few dozen workers to run a distillery; now it just takes a few.

As a result of these changes, the single malt distillers began looking for a new market for their whisky. "Single malt at the end of the day provides you with more profit," says Ian Millar, the Global Brand Ambassador for William Grant & Sons, which makes Glenfiddich, the number one single malt in the world. "Sales of our single malt grew to the point where eventually, other whisky companies realized that this was not just a fad but a real business opportunity, and so the category became more established with the introduction of other malt whiskies." It was a genius idea, because not only were the distillers able to find a new market for their whisky, but they were able to get consumers to pay a premium for it. Single malt whisky acquired the reputation of being much better and sophisticated than blends, which helped to drive its sales. (A similar strategy is now being used by some coffee brands, which are selling high-priced coffee that comes from a single estate. Traditionally these beans would have been blended with coffee from other estates.)

During the 1980s, many single malts started to appear on American shelves, including for the first time brands like Macallan, Oban, Talisker, and Lagavulin. But many of the early malts that came to America, according to Hansell, were pretty unexciting. One reason was that the distillers were used to making whisky to be used by blenders and not consumed straight. It took some time for the different distilleries to find their niche and perfect their flavor. But by the early 1990s, the popularity of the spirit began to grow and has continued to increase ever since. "No one predicted that Scotch whisky would be this popular," says Hansell. Over the last five to seven years, overall supply has tightened, and single malt prices have shot up.

Drinkers have developed an appreciation and connoisseurship of single malts. During the past few years, "People who got into single malt are ignoring 10- and 12-year-olds and are trading up," says Glenfiddich's Millar. To satisfy this new need, the whisky companies

John Glaser: Whisky Pioneer

An independent seeks to shake up the staid and corporate world of Scotch whisky.

John Glaser is a maverick in the Scotch whisky world, but he almost became a winemaker. After completing college, he worked in different parts of the wine business, even spending time in Burgundy, and he considered enrolling at University of California—Davis to study winemaking. He decided against it after realizing the course load included a lot of chemistry.

In 1994, Glaser took a job in New York with Diageo to work on Johnnie Walker whisky. At the time, "I knew nothing about Scotch whisky," he admits. He figured that someday he might be able to switch over to the wines in Diageo's portfolio. When he arrived in Scotland for the first time to visit the distilleries, he expected to see giant, ugly factories pumping out whisky. Instead, he was charmed by the beauty and history of the industry and the distilleries, which date back hundreds of years. "The wheels started spinning," he says. By 1998, he was working in Johnnie Walker's office in London and building contacts in the Scotch industry.

Glaser says he had discovered that whisky was "a pretty staid and traditional business." In the back of his mind, ideas began to take shape about how to improve its production and marketing. He approached Diageo with the idea of creating a boutique blended whisky company. They passed on the idea, and Glaser left to form his own craft blending company, which he called Compass Box Whisky. It was a gutsy move, because as he admits, it's "a business dominated by a small number of companies." In 2000, Glaser blended the first batch of whisky in his kitchen. Since the company's humble beginning, Compass Box has released a number of innovative and interesting whiskies, including the all-grain Hedonism and the super-smoky Peat Monster. Glaser is rethinking all aspects of the whisky business, including label design and the quality of the cask in which the whisky is aged. "There are so many interesting things we can do," he says. "It's time to accelerate the evolution."

But the industry isn't always ready for his ideas or products. For instance, Compass Box put out a whisky called The Spice Tree. Glaser blended a number of single malts (technically this blend is called a "vatted malt" because it doesn't contain grain whisky) and aged the spirit a second time in casks made with high-end French oak inserts. The Scotch Whisky Association didn't approve of the process and asked Glaser to stop producing the spirit. (Without the Association's approval, the blend can't be called Scotch whisky.)

But not all the attention on Glaser's whiskies has been negative. *Food & Wine* chose his Asyla as its best whisky of the year in 2002. In 2002 and 2003, *Malt Advocate Magazine* called Glaser "Pioneer of the Year," and *Whisky Magazine* has named him "Innovator of the Year" three times. All of these accolades are well deserved, because Glaser's innovations are helping to reshape the Scotch industry.

quickly expanded their product lines to include older and more varied offerings. In 1997 and 1998, Highland Park introduced its now acclaimed 15-, 18-, and 25-year-old single malt whiskies. In 1996, Glenmorangie introduced its line of "Wood Finishes." The whisky is aged in the traditional manner in old bourbon casks and then is finished in barrels that formerly held wine or sherry. Even the blends have introduced more expensive line extensions. Chivas Regal asked master blender Colin Scott to come up with the company's first ever 18-year-old blend. (One reason the company decided on making an 18-year-old was that the number is considered lucky in its targeted Asian cultures.) Johnnie Walker introduced its super-high-end Blue in 1992. Even the Famous Grouse, known for its easy-drinking blend, launched a $35 12-year-old and a $55 18-year-old blended malt whisky in the fall of 2005. This rapid response was quite remarkable given the fact that the distillers had only recently begun to bottle whisky for consumers.

An auction market for vintage single malt has also developed and is thriving. According to Martin Green, a vintage whisky expert and consultant at McTear's auction house in Glasgow, Scotland, the first auction to feature whisky was held by Christie's in 1983. McTear's held the first all-whisky auction in 1989. To get an idea of how popular whisky collecting has become, consider that McTear's now holds four whisky auctions each year. "People buying ten years ago now want to sell," says Green. "They've realized it's a form of investment." And prices are rising for these bottles. The benchmark is Macallan, arguably the favorite of whisky collectors because of its quality and the availability of vintage bottles. From 1996 to 2006 at auction, the price of a bottle of the brand's 1926, 60-year-old whisky has more than doubled.

The whisky companies took note of this trend and began to dig through their cellars to release special rare bottlings. These limited edition whiskies have created excitement among collectors as well as drawn considerable attention from the general public. In 1999, The Glenlivet started a Cellar Collection program, which periodically releases limited editions of extremely special and expensive spirits. For instance, in 2004, the company released just over 1,800 bottles of a 1964 whisky. The 800 bottles allocated for the U.S. market were each priced at $2,000. As of fall 2006, there had been six different special bottlings in the company's Cellar Collection. Not to be outdone, in April of 2002, Macallan launched the most ambitious vintage whisky program yet: the Fine & Rare Collection. It launched with 10,000 bottles and 37 distinctive vintages covering over 116 years with a value at the time of $20 million The company says they released the collection because "it is expected to appeal to the growing segment of enthusiasts who are fascinated by the intricacies of old whiskies, to drink or collect." (Macallan even released a book about the collection and the vintage whisky auction market.)

Many more distilleries have released rare and pricey bottles to tap into this demand. For example, Glenrothes, which for a long time only went into blends like Cutty Sark, came out with a pricey bottling of a single 1979 cask (cask #13458) in the fall of 2006. Each of the 519 bottles was priced at $1,000. And some blenders have also introduced extremely rare offerings. To celebrate Johnnie Walker's anniversary, the brand released a limited edition cask-strength version of its already pricey Blue Label. The special spirit came in a squat square Baccarat decanter, which was enclosed in a blue leather case. Each of the anniversary packs sold for $3,500—that is, if you could find a store that still had it in stock.

With the popularity of single malts on the rise, a number of distilleries that had been mothballed reopened, including Bruichladdich, Scapa, and Benromach. And with demand so high, many distillers have cut back the amount of whisky they sell to blenders. Some have even gone further. Since the early 1990s, Glenmorangie stopped selling its whisky to blenders and now bottles all of its single malt. Further proof that single malt whisky has gone from being a curiosity to a bar staple is that distilleries are now licensing their name. For instance, Edelman Leather, which supplies Herman Miller, now makes a Glenlivet Chair whose color matches the brand's 21-year-old whisky. And just as restaurants have offered special dinners showcasing a particular wine variety or vintage, there are now whisky dinners. The Fairmont Miramar Hotel in Santa Monica, California, for instance, put together a five-course, $100-per-person Macallan dinner in 2006. Not to mention the success of *Malt*

On the Whisky Trail

For years, oenophiles have made the pilgrimage to Napa and Sonoma to see where their favorite wines are made. The vineyard has become a key component of a wine brand's marketing plan. Many of these wineries are designed to welcome visitors, with gift shops, tasting rooms, and restaurants. Something similar is happening in Scotland. As single malt whiskies have become more popular, an increasing number of drinkers have started to visit the Scottish Whisky Trail, which runs through the Speyside section of the Highlands. About four hours north of Edinburgh, the Trail is made up of some of the most famous distilleries in the world. Taking a cue from the wine industry, the distilleries have begun to turn themselves into bona fide tourist attractions, with introductory movies, cafés, and even in-depth "connoisseur" tours for serious whisky fans. Here are some highlights on the Whisky Trail.

The Glenlivet

Located in a beautiful spot in the highlands, The Glenlivet is surrounded by soaring mountains where flocks of sure-footed sheep graze. The distillery was the first in 1824 to be licensed by the government and ever since has been making some of the best-known whisky in the world. The distillery has a large visitor's center with a new exhibition about the brand, a gift shop, and a café. Visitors can also take a complimentary tour of the facility, which ends with a dram of the 12- or 18-year-old.

Glenfiddich

The number one selling Scottish whisky in the world is located just a mile outside of Dufftown, the heart of the region. Before a free tour of the facility, visitors are treated to a dramatic short movie about the William Grant family and the founding of the company made by Hollywood director Ridley Scott. There's a café and a gift shop, and the distillery also offers a two-and-a-half-hour connoisseur's tour (about $40) that ends with a whisky tasting. Glenfiddich's sister brand, Balvenie, located just next door, also offers tours. The tour takes about two and a half hours and costs about $40. Reservations are required.

Macallan

Until recently, Macallan didn't publicize its location in an effort to discourage people from visiting. The policy wasn't enacted out of elitism but necessity. The layout of the distillery isn't conducive for tours. But to satisfy its fans, the company recently built a gift shop and a large exhibit space on the second floor of one its whisky warehouses. Currently it's filled with a display about the wood used in constructing the brand's barrels. The company offers both a regular tour (about $10) and a Precious Tour (about $30). Both tours end with a tasting. For Macallan fans, the gift shop offers limited edition, seasonal, single-cask bottlings that aren't available anywhere else. It also sells rare vintages, like an eight-year-old, that are made for various export markets.

Speyside Cooperage

One hundred years ago, most whisky companies employed coopers to fix and maintain their casks. But for reasons of space and economy, most whisky brands now no longer employ their own coopers. Instead they use large commercial cooperages like the Speyside Cooperage, located four miles outside of Dufftown, which

(continued)

makes or fixes about 100,000 casks per year for a number of different whisky brands. The cooperage is open to visitors who can watch the coopers at work from a viewing balcony. Admission costs about $6 for adults.

The Quaich Bar at the Craigellachie Hotel

One of the best places to taste whisky is the legendary Quaich Bar at the Craigellachie Hotel. (The bar's name comes from the traditional Celtic two-handled drinking bowl.) Even though the Quaich is small with only a few tables, the walls are covered in shelves holding more than 700 bottles of single malt whisky. The well-versed bartenders are more than willing to make recommendations and help you navigate the thick menu. You can find whiskies that sell for just a few dollars a glass, but rare malts can fetch up to $530 a drink.

Advocate's annual WhiskyFest. This veritable whisky mecca allows fans to taste over 200 whiskies and meet with company representatives. The event started in New York in 1998, where it sells out every year, and now also takes place in Chicago and San Francisco.

At this point, the future of single malt looks bright, and it's hard to imagine that the category won't continue to grow. Over the past few years, distillers have been able to attract increasingly sophisticated drinkers by offering ever more complex and interesting spirits at higher prices. Single malts and expensive blends have been turned into status symbols, not unlike imported chocolate, high-priced designer jeans, and artisanal cheeses, with a loyal and wealthy following. For many whisky brands, higher prices and more limited supply means increased demand. These expensive bottles have helped the rest of the industry to introduce premium and super-premium spirits.

One advantage that the Scotch industry has over many of the other spirits categories is the high cost of starting a new single malt brand. Not only are distilleries expensive to build, but the whisky has to be made in Scotland and aged for at least three years, usually much longer. A new brand would take more than a decade to start from scratch. Comparatively, vodka is relatively cheap and fast to produce. It's no surprise, then, that entrepreneurs are attracted to the white unaged spirit. As a result, the big Scotch brands don't have to worry too much about new competition or the market's becoming saturated with whisky. However, because worldwide demand is increasing rapidly, many distilleries are running at full capacity, and some are even expanding. But the effects of this increased production won't be felt for a while. Remember, most of the whisky made today won't hit shelves for at least another 12 years.

Still, the spirits business tends to be cyclical. Over the last 180 years, the whisky industry has gone through a number of booms and busts. Some experts are now afraid that with prices so high, consumers may ultimately lose interest and buy less expensive whisky. (To be fair, the recent weakness of the dollar has also helped push Scotch prices up.) According to Hansell, for many years, single malts were undervalued compared to cognac, and you could find a good bottle for under $20. "Now the gap's closing," he says. "The bargain now is bourbon. You can get a good bottle for under $15." And for whisky drinkers, a price correction wouldn't be a bad thing. "I'm hoping prices will be slashed," admits Hansell. "They've gone up a lot the last five years."

Courtesy of Pernod Ricard USA

Vodka
Straight Up

. . . .

FROM ABOVE, COGNAC, France, looks like an intricate quilt of geometrically striped green-and-light-brown patches. Closer to the ground, each patch reveals itself to be a field of crops or tight rows of trained grape vines. Old chateaus and crumbling farm houses dot the landscape, giving the area the feel of a perfect Hollywood set. The grapes, of course, are cultivated for the area's world-famous eponymous spirit. The small town, made up of old, low, light-colored stone buildings, is still centered around producing cognac, and it's hard to avoid the proud displays of bottles in shop windows or the cognac distilleries themselves. The warehouses are covered in a black patina of mold generated by the aging cognac, which the town wears as a badge of honor, proof that the spirit is still made the same way as it was hundreds of years ago.

But just outside the town, on a dusty road that winds through the fields, is a large, new, and unremarkable gray structure that from a distance looks like a large airplane hangar. But the hulking building is the home of another famous spirit: Grey Goose Vodka. To the surprise of many drinkers, one of the world's best-known vodkas isn't made in Russia, Poland, or Scandinavia but in this quiet southwestern corner of France. Inside the mirrored front doors (which feature two oversized *G*s as handles) is a small reception area complete with four flat-screen TVs and loud, piped-in techno pop. Set into the floor is a glass cube filled with crushed glass and Grey Goose bottles. The room has the feel of an exclusive nightclub thousands of miles away in Miami or New York, where bottles of the brand's vodka are sold for hundreds of dollars each.

Inside the massive facility are huge stainless steel tanks made for the pharmaceutical industry that hold thousands of liters of vodka which is actually produced in a distillery in Central France. And at the center of the building is a highly mechanized, state-of-the-art bottling facility, which for the most part runs on it own. Workers feed the line pallets of empty bottles. Machines fill the bottles, fold the boxes, and package the spirit. At the other end are pallets of neatly stacked cases of vodka that are covered in plastic wrap ready for shipping. The whole process takes about five minutes when both lines are functioning, and the plant can produce up to 16,000 bottles an hour. It's hard to talk over the hum of the machines and the incessant ding of bottles bumping gently against each other.

The finished vodka is picked up by a small forklift and brought into a giant storeroom with aisles upon aisles of towering stacks of fully loaded palates. It feels like a Costco, except there's only one product for sale. Most of the finished bottles go into large shipping containers destined for the United States, where 94 percent of the vodka is consumed. The vodka is hard to find even in the local bars and disco.

At first, it seems odd that this oversized monument to modern technology would be built in the middle of the French countryside, where distilling traditions and techniques predate the discovery of the New World. But it's no accident that the brand has always been located in Cognac. For one thing, the area has an excellent supply of water that is naturally filtered through Champagne limestone, and the townspeople have inherited hundreds of years of distilling expertise. But most importantly, coming from France also makes the vodka unique. It was one of the first vodkas made in France to be exported to the United States. And the French origins lend a certain *je ne sais quoi* or flair of luxury to the brand. Those ingredients are absolutely necessary to create a super-premium spirit, especially when that product was dreamed up in prosaic New Rochelle, New York, and costs $30 a bottle. In Eastern Europe, vodka "used to be a peasants' drink," says Aleco Azqueta, group marketing manager of Grey Goose. But his brand gave the spirit "the French spin, the luxury spin, and the culinary spin."

Thanks to Grey Goose and its competitors, vodka has become a luxury product, which seemingly can never be premium enough. The clear alcohol, which by definition has a neutral taste, is the fastest-growing, largest segment of the spirits business. In 2005, 761 different vodkas were for sale, an increase of almost 56 percent from 2000 according to the Distilled Spirits Council of the United States (DISCUS). But vodka is still relatively new to America. People really started drinking the spirit in the 1950s, but for years, it lagged behind whisky and the other "white spirits," gin and rum. In 1952, according to DISCUS, vodka sales made up just 1 percent of total industry volume. The spirit got a boost from Ian Fleming, whose character James Bond ordered a vodka cocktail, the Vesper, in the 1953 book *Casino Royale.* Bond also orders his famous vodka martini "shaken, not stirred" in the 1962 hit movie *Dr. No.* By 1970, on the strength of Smirnoff's successful "it leaves you breathless" advertising campaign and the rise in popularity of cocktails, especially the Moscow Mule, the spirit surpassed gin. Just five years later, vodka overtook the blended whisky category.

Vodka hasn't looked back. In 2005, vodka made up over 27 percent of total industry sales. To put that impressive performance in perspective, all the whisky categories combined made up just over 26 percent of industry sales. In 2005, Smirnoff, the number one vodka in the world, sold over 25 million nine-liter cases, up 3 percent from the previous year. The sales volume was so large, it was good enough to make Smirnoff the top-selling premium distilled spirit.

But until the 1980s, drinkers had few vodka brands from which to choose except the domestically produced Smirnoff, Russian Stolichnaya (Stoli, for short), the Scandinavian Finlandia, and a few value brands. The first imported vodka, Stoli, was introduced to the U.S. market as recently as 1965. (One reason it succeeded was that in 1973, Pepsico agreed to trade Pepsi for the vodka, which it then distributed around the country.) Only over the last 25 years has the category exploded, filling stores and bars with ever pricier and more exotic bottles from all over the world. Not only are there bottles from traditional powerhouses like Russia, Poland, and Sweden but from upstarts like France, New Zealand, and even Iceland, which had never produced a vodka until 2005. The launch of Absolut in 1979 and its now-famous ad campaign paved the way for these new high-end vodkas.

This alcohol is a dream for spirit companies because vodka can be made out of virtually anything and is relatively cheap to manufacture. Vodka has been made in Russia and Poland since about the 12th century from rye, wheat, and potatoes. But these days, many vodka companies don't actually distill their spirit from scratch. Many American brands buy neutral grain spirit from a big Midwestern company like Archer Daniels Midland, which makes the alcohol in a huge commercial column still. The individual vodka company redistills the neutral grain spirit or combines it with a homemade eau-de-vie or adds a flavor. The spirit is usually then filtered before it is bottled. What makes vodka production especially appealing is that, unlike whisky, the spirit doesn't need to be aged. Aging is expensive because producers have to wait years, if not decades, to sell the product and in the meantime pay for storage. Furthermore, as a spirit ages, some of it seeps out of the cask and evaporates into the atmosphere (called the "angel's share"), reducing the number of bottles that can be sold. "The nice thing about vodka is, you make it today, you sell it tomorrow; even Jagermeister is aged for a year," said Sidney Frank, the father of Grey Goose, in a 2005 interview with *Inc.* magazine. "So you don't have to put your money into buildings and machines and warehouses."

To justify higher prices and profits, vodka companies have invested in higher-quality ingredients—and more exotic backstories. Most vodka brands don't have the rich history or the ancient distilling practices of a single malt Scotch whisky. How extreme has this history-writing trend become? Makers of the Polish vodka Belvedere send the spirit back and forth to the 16th-century French town of Collonges-la-Rouge to be flavored before it's bottled and shipped. Vodka companies have also given their bottles a luxury makeover. Bottle design can now be a lengthy and expensive part of creating a brand. For example, the Danish Danzka comes in an aluminum shaker-shaped bottle that supposedly chills faster than a traditional glass bottle. And the single-estate Polish rye vodka Wyborowa hired celebrity architect Frank Gehry to design a distinctive skyscraper-like bottle that bears his name.

Vodka companies have also spent a lot on advertising campaigns that promote the taste of their spirit. At first, this might seem odd—vodka is supposed to have a neutral flavor. Yet the strategy has been very successful for a number of companies. After Grey Goose took top honors in a Beverage Testing Institute vodka tasting, the company used its first $3 million in profits to buy ads (many in *The Wall Street Journal*) touting itself as the world's best-tasting vodka. This claim, plus the attractive bottle, was enough to convince many consumers to buy the spirit. Pravda Vodka is currently running full-page ads promoting itself as the best vodka because it was selected as the top luxury vodka at the 2004 World Beverage Championships in San Francisco. Part of the company's campaign is to send out free tasting kits to consumers who want to compare the spirit to their usual vodka of choice. Today there are so many different tasting events and championships, many spirit companies can claim to be the best, featuring gold medals on their labels. It's hard to believe that consumers still pay attention to these claims.

Driving the growth of vodka are two major phenomena: the demand for super-premium bottlings and added flavoring. The vodka category has always been about luxury and raising the bar. The key to Absolut's success was its high price tag and air of luxury. According to Stoli, the company actually introduced the first so-called super-premium vodka way back in 1989 called Cristall, whose name was later changed to Stolichanaya Gold. But over the last few years, the race to develop ever more expensive and distinctive products has really heated up. Just a few years ago, the price for vodka topped out at about $17 for Absolut. That increased to $30 with the debut of Grey Goose, Chopin, and Belvedere in the late 1990s. Now the market is flooded with $30 vodkas, which don't seem all that expensive anymore. The top shelf is now reserved for a number of vodkas that sell for $60 or above, including Stoli Elit and fashion designer Roberto Cavalli's eponymous vodka. As a result, even Absolut, the number one imported vodka, has seen its market share decline. To keep up with the rest of the industry, the company introduced the higher-priced Level vodka brand (about $30 a bottle) in March 2004.

With all these product introductions, it makes sense that in the short period between 2002 and 2005, the number of cases of super-premium vodka sold increased by over 90 percent according to DISCUS. For all premium vodka categories combined over the same period, case sales increased by more than 23 percent, while case sales of value vodka only increased by 9 percent. Arguably vodkas like Absolut, Stoli, and Grey Goose created the concept and market for

Sidney Frank: The Master Marketer
The man behind Grey Goose, Jagermeister, and the ultra-premium spirits phenomenon

Sidney Frank's life story reads like a fairy tale. Born just after the end of World War I, he grew up poor on a farm in Montville, Connecticut, sleeping, he claimed, on sheets made from old flour sacks. When he died in 2006, he was a billionaire.

Frank's uniquely American meteoric rise culminated in the sale of the Grey Goose vodka brand, which he created from scratch just seven years earlier, to Bacardi for over $2 billion. But he wasn't ready to retire. He told *BusinessWeek*, "I'd like to be the $10 billion man." Before his death, he was working on projects like the Corazon tequila brand, a travel magazine, an Irish whiskey, and the Crunk energy drink that he created with rapper Lil' John.

Frank got into the liquor business unintentionally. He attended Brown University for a year, crediting his admission to the fact that he impressed a university official with his strong handshake. He had saved enough money for his freshman year's tuition by working odd jobs. When he arrived in Rhode Island, he was assigned to live with Edward Sarnoff, son of David Sarnoff, then president of RCA. Frank's time at Brown was short-lived, and he was forced to leave school because he didn't have enough money to continue. (After selling Grey Goose, he gave the school the largest donation it has ever received: a $100 million gift for scholarships and another $20 million for an academic building.) But through his Brown acquaintances, Frank got to know Louise "Skippy" Rosenstiel, who—after six proposals—agreed to marry him. Her father was head of Schenley Distilleries, a huge player in the spirits industry. After a

(continued)

stint working for Pratt & Whitney, he joined the family business at Schenley and ultimately became the company's president. He took credit for the success of Ancient Age and Dewar's White Label. But it wasn't a smooth ride to the top, and after his wife's death and a fight with the Rosenstiel family, he quit.

First he sold art, and then, in 1972, he joined with his brother Eugene to create Sidney Frank Importing. The brothers began by supplying Japanese restaurants with Gekkeikan Sake. The first few years weren't easy, and Frank sold off property and art to keep the company afloat. But in 1974, he found the German liqueur Jagermeister in a bar in New York's Yorkville neighborhood. Frank was intrigued, and soon he began importing the unique, herbal-flavored spirit. Sales were relatively slow until 1985, when Jager-meister was discovered by Louisiana State University students and soon became the drink of choice for college kids across the country. It didn't hurt that the *Baton Rogue Advocate* called it "liquid Valium" and the spirit was rumored to be an aphrodisiac. To capital-ize on this turn of events, Frank hired models, whom he dubbed "Jagerettes" and later "Jagerdudes," and sent them to bars to hand out promotional literature and get people to try a sample. Frank also invented a special tap that would pour a refrigerated shot of super-cool Jager, which made it even more palatable. In 1974, he had sold approximately 600 cases of Jagermeister. According to the *New York Times,* he sold 1.3 million cases in 2005.

But Frank wasn't satisfied with his Jagermeister success. In 1997, he decided to launch a vodka that would steal the premium market from Absolut. At the time, the Swedish vodka dominated the market at the then-extravagant price of $15 to $17 a bottle. Frank decided that he would sell his vodka for $30, increasing his profit margin and lending the spirit an air of exclusivity and desirability.

He told *Forbes,* "Vodka is just water and alcohol, so if I sold a bottle for $30, the $10 difference is almost all profit."

He correctly predicted that the market was ready for a premium category of spirits. With the beginning of the dot-com bubble, his timing couldn't have been better. To bolster the image of luxury, the vodka was packaged in a fancy frosted bottle with a reverse label that he claimed to have designed himself. (At first, it was also shipped in wooden crates.) To give it an air of sophistication, he based the brand in Cognac, France. Frank used the first year's profits to pay for advertising. For example, he ran countless ads in *The Wall Street Journal* after Grey Goose won a top prize at a 1998 vodka tasting. He also gave away bottles to charities and awards shows and made sure that bars got a jumbo-sized bottle to display prominently. Frank's untraditional marketing plan worked, of course. Before the Bacardi deal, Frank was selling 1.4 million cases of Grey Goose each year. And the brand's success became the game plan for countless entrepreneurs. But Frank knew the spirit had definitely arrived when Carrie Bradshaw and the rest of the *Sex and the City* characters ordered their cosmos made with Grey Goose.

all premium spirits. Thanks to these high-end spirits, people actually started specifying the brand of alcohol they want in their mixed drinks. The high-end vodkas have also led the rest of the industry to develop luxury bottles and are the key reason why all spirits have enjoyed a renaissance.

Another explanation for the success of high-priced vodkas is nightclub bottle service. Around the country, clubs have instituted a policy that requires patrons who want to get in or sit down at a table on a popular night to buy a bottle or two of alcohol. (Mixers and ice are included in the price.) The clubs, of course, mark up the price of the bottles extravagantly. It's not unheard of for a $30 bottle of Grey Goose to go for nearly $400. To be fair, clubs are often filled with people who monopolize a table all night only to buy a couple of drinks. According to David Rabin, president of the New York Nightlife Association, he was reluctant to introduce the policy in Lotus, his popular club, but he did so "because it became a real estate issue." There were only so many tables in his club, and he "needed to figure out a way to 'earn' from our prime real estate."

Club patrons aren't just getting a bottle but also a level of status. "When you're sitting down, you want people to see what you're drinking," says Azqueta. Why? When you go out, "subconsciously there's always the need to impress." According to *New York Magazine*, the policy was practically unheard of in the United States before 1993. But with the dot-com bubble came plenty of young people flush with cash and looking to impress each other. To take advantage of the trend, clubs and lounges around New York City began to institute bottle service. The policy soon was adopted by clubs in Miami and Las Vegas. By 2006, according to the magazine, there were seven clubs with bottle service just on 27th Street in the Chelsea section of Manhattan. And like a popular dance (or cocktail), this phenomenon has spread across the country. According to a story in *Fortune* magazine, clubs in more than 15 cities, including Indianapolis, Toledo, and Milwaukee, now offer bottle service.

In addition to the profits at stake, clubs like bottle service because it controls the crowds and minimizes the demand on the bar staff. Plus, "Customers like it a lot in that they don't have to wait for a waitress to fight through the crowd and also they can make their own drinks," says Rabin. And just as at New York's famous power broker lunch spot the Four Seasons restaurant, in many clubs the same people book the same table every weekend. This allows a club to forecast accurately the size of a night's crowd and anticipate how many bottles they'll sell. Although these clubs stock many types of alcohol, vodka and champagne are usually the most popular and dominate the menus. "When you're buying a bottle for $300, you want something that everyone can enjoy," says Azqueta. Clearly, vodka is a pretty safe choice compared to whisky, which is an acquired taste. As a result, bottle service has helped create vodka's luxury image.

It's not just vodka's high price tag that's attracting customers but also what's actually in the bottles. The other major trend driving vodka sales is flavoring. You can now buy vodkas flavored with vanilla, orange, pomegranate, blueberry, pepper, green tea, and even wasabi. According to the Adams Beverage Group, in 2005 vodka makers introduced 21 new flavored vodkas. But that's actually down from 2003, when 27 new flavored vodkas were introduced.

While the rest of the world prefers vodka unadulterated, Americans can't get enough of the flavored spirit. In fact, most of the major vodka manufacturers offer at least three flavors, generally orange, lemon, and vanilla. Some of the companies have gone much further and offer a veritable cornucopia. The Dutch vodka Van Gogh offers a remarkable 14 flavors, from "double espresso" (with caffeine) to mango to mojito mint. In 2005, Absolut reportedly spent $15 million on its "Find Your Flavor" advertising campaign to highlight the brand's selection of vodkas. The company's website even offered a 90-second quiz to find the vodka you best matched; based on the findings, the site could spit out a personal cocktail recipe for you, using that flavor.

Flavored vodkas have been around for decades—Stoli introduced a pepper vodka and a honey vodka in 1971—but the momentum was slow to build. Arguably the first successful flavored vodka was Absolut Peppar, launched in 1986. In the late 1990s, flavored vodkas really began to take off at the same time as the rebirth of the

Vodka Boutique

The biggest vodka brands sell millions of cases every year. Smirnoff alone sells over 25 million. But there are now an increasing number of small boutique distillers across the country. These artisanal vodkas are sometimes hard to find but are definitely worth tracking down and tasting. Unlike the industry giants, these smaller brands can experiment with unique ingredients and use old-fashioned distilling techniques. Here are five of the best boutique vodkas on the market.

Charbay

These days, all the major vodka manufacturers offer a wide array of flavors. But Charbay was one of the first companies to produce more than just a standard orange or vanilla vodka. The company's vodka is infused with particularly flavorful varieties of fruit, like blood orange, Meyer lemon, key lime, and ruby red grapefruit. Unlike its competitors, Charbay macerates the whole fruit to flavor its vodka. The amount of each spirit that the company can produce is limited because it only uses fruit when it's in season.

Tito's

Even though Texas has a beer and whiskey reputation, Austin's Tito's Handmade Vodka could change all that. The company is the state's first licensed distillery, and the vodka is distilled six times for an extra-smooth taste. The brand was founded by a former geologist, Tito Beveridge, and has won numerous awards. Beveridge even built the company's first pot still from spare parts. "I had no idea if it would work," he says. Not bad for a company that broke 100,000 cases for the first time in 2005. Tito admits the brand is "a lot bigger than I ever thought."

Square One

It's hard to go grocery shopping these days without filling up your cart with organic products. But not until the summer of 2006 did the first domestically produced organic rye vodka hit the market. Square One is made from organically grown North Dakota rye and water from the Snake River in Wyoming's Teton Range. The vodka is fermented naturally and is made in a four-column continuous still before being charcoal filtered.

Hangar One

One of the world's best-flavored vodkas is made in a World War II era hangar on an old air base in northern California. The brand was created by Ansley Coale and Jorg Rupf, who are well known for their own boutique spirit companies. Hangar One takes quality vodka produced on a column still and then redistills it in a European pot still. The company produces a fine straight vodka and four different flavored vodkas, including the citrus Buddha's Hand, Kaffir Lemon, and Fraser River Raspberry.

Dogfish Head

Already well known for their unique and experimental craft beers, the Delaware-based Dogfish Head has branched out into microdistilling. The company makes a number of spirits, including the 80-proof charcoal-filtered Blue Hen Vodka. The distillery also produces an array of interesting seasonal vodka infusions. In the past, they've offered garlic, dark chocolate, and guava vodkas. Unfortunately, the spirits are only distributed to a handful of states, but they are available at the company's distillery and at its brewpub in Maryland.

cocktail. These two trends weren't coincidental; rather, they fed off of each other. White spirits have always been praised for how easily they work in mixed drinks. "Vodka is so easy to work with," says Julie Reiner, co-owner of two of New York City's finest cocktail bars, the Flatiron Lounge and the Pegu Club. But it's almost too easy: "Once you become advanced in mixology, it becomes boring to work with vodka," she says.

The spirit quickly became a favorite of bartenders and customers, who ordered vodka-based cocktails in droves, especially cosmopolitans and apple martinis. Both drinks are often made with flavored vodkas. A flavored vodka can add another taste element to a drink, and vodka manufacturers have hired mixologists and celebrities to develop special cocktail recipes that call for a flavored spirit to entice both customers and bartenders. (Flavored vodka can also be a shortcut for the bartender, eliminating one step in the mixing process. No need to add orange juice for example, if the vodka already is orange flavored.) Some of the best mixologists have started making their own flavored vodka by infusing the plain spirit with fruits or spices.

For the home bartender, flavored vodkas have been a major boon. You don't need to be a trained bartender to make a decent-tasting screwdriver or a Cape Cod (cranberry and vodka). But it's even easier to fix a drink if the vodka is already flavored. Many people now forsake adding anything but club soda to a jigger of flavored vodka. Not only does it pack a high alcohol punch with some flavor, but it is also a relatively low-calorie cocktail. Simple vodka cocktails are an alternative to drinks like the mojito or caipirinha, which are usually loaded with sugar, and vodka companies are now using this angle to promote their products. For example, Skyy Vodka's website highlights its nutritional properties. For calorie-conscience consumers, the company offers a table listing the number of calories, fats, total carbohydrates, and proteins in a single serving of its vodka.

The Famous Face of High-End Spirits
Make mine an Ed McMahon on the rocks.

Over the last few years, the fastest-growing area of the spirits business has been the high-end and super-premium categories. Companies have successfully convinced consumers to trade up to more luxurious and glamorous (pricier) products. These campaigns have worked so well that some bona fide celebrities have come out with their own spirit labels.

This practice is long established in the wine world. Francis Ford Coppola bought his winery in 1975. Since then, a constellation of other stars, including Sting, Bob Dylan, Olivia Newton John, Greg Norman, and Emeril Lagasse, have entered the winemaking business. Even adult film star Savanna Samson introduced a wine that has scored high marks from Robert Parker. And don't overlook Marilyn Wines, named for Marilyn Monroe, whose bottles bear photos of the actress on the label.

About ten years ago, celebrities began branding their own spirits. One of the first was Sammy Hagar's Blue Agave Cabo Wabo Tequila. The Red Rocker's spirit hit shelves in 1996, and sales in 2006 were up by 30 percent over the previous year. Willie Nelson came out with Old Whiskey River bourbon, inspired by one of his famous songs. The bottle even comes decorated with a real guitar pick. Roc-A-Fella Records, the rap label created by Damon Dash and Jay-Z, released Armadale vodka in 2002. According to the company's website, the label had looked into a deal promoting Belvedere vodka because rap music had been responsible for the popularity of a number of brands in the "urban community." Ultimately the company decided to put out its own vodka.

(continued)

Enticed by the potential profits, the number of celebrity bottlings has significantly increased over the last few years. In the spring
of 2006 alone, fashion designer Roberto Cavalli, Ed McMahon, and
even teetotaler Donald Trump came out with vodkas. (It's no surprise
that vodka is so popular because it is relatively fast, easy, and cheap
to make and requires no aging.) There is also a trend towards naming spirits after deceased celebrities. There's a Frida Kahlo tequila,
which bears the image of the popular Mexican artist on its label.
And there's now a line of spirits called Hendrix Electric after rock
musician and cult icon Jimi Hendrix; the bottles feature his photo.
Surely, this is only the beginning of the trend. It doesn't take much
imagination to conjure up a Snoop Dogg gin-and-juice drink.

But not all flavored vodkas are made the same way. Traditionally in Russia, people flavored their own vodka by infusing it with
pieces of fruit or perhaps a horseradish root. (The popular midtown
Manhattan bar, The Russian Vodka Room, features almost a dozen
homemade infused vodkas.) But these sorts of infusions don't keep
for very long and can't be bottled. The best vodka producers buy
fruit and spices from famous growing regions, such as lemons from
Menton, France, and vanilla from Madagascar. The distillers juice or
macerate the whole fruit, skin and all. The spirit is then infused with
ground-up fruit and finally distilled again. Other vodka makers add
a natural fruit essence before or after the final distillation. Artificial
flavoring or sugar syrups are also often used. There is "such amazing technology in terms of flavoring agents," says Stoli senior brand
manager Adam Rosen. (For the record, Stoli uses natural juices to
flavor their vodkas.) This is one reason why cheaper value brands
have also been able to offer flavored vodkas.

With so many flavored vodkas on the market, can this craze continue? The short answer is no. Most experts agree that flavored vodkas have established themselves as a bar staple. But "not every vodka brand can sustain a family of flavored vodkas," says Rosen. As the novelty wears off, it won't be a surprise if some companies discontinue certain flavors. That seems far off, though, especially because vodka makers have devoted considerable resources to developing new flavors that will hit the market over the next few years. So no need to stock up on the wasabi vodka.

Certainly the overall premium vodka category is still quite healthy, and prices will continue to climb. Vodka manufacturers have skillfully dominated the industry by turning the spirit into a status symbol—not an easy thing to do, considering there is nothing romantic about how vodka is made. But consumers were convinced by slick marketing and high prices that vodka was particularly exotic and valuable. The vodka companies then bolstered their appeal by using flavorings, which made the spirit more palatable and attracted new drinkers. (The variety and quality of the flavorings became yet another selling point.) These efforts have been so successful that they have been copied by other spirit categories.

Vodka's meteoric rise in popularity was quite a feat but not unprecedented. Companies in other industries have successfully employed similar tactics. One famous example is the flood of premium foreign-sounding ice creams that overtook supermarkets in the early 1980s. Consumers were impressed by these pseudo-Scandinavian products, which, despite their names, were in fact made domestically and had little or no connection to Europe. For example, even though the Häagen-Dazs's pints bore a map of Denmark, the brand was dreamed up by Reuben Mattus, a Polish immigrant who started out selling ice cream in the Bronx. These companies also invested a lot of money in creating eye-catching and distinctive packaging for their products. Frusen Glädjé came in a futuristic,

Spirited Advertising

From the Absolut ad campaign to the world's best tasting vodka to spirits going prime time

These days, it's hard to read a magazine, watch TV, listen to the radio, or even ride the New York City subway without seeing an ad for a spirits brand. And it's no wonder, because the industry spends hundreds of millions of dollars every year trying to get your attention. With sales of spirits growing each year, this strategy seems to have paid off handsomely. But a memorable series of ads can not only pump up sales but also turn a bottle into an icon and a brand into a household name. The most successful campaigns transcend mere marketing and actually affect not only what consumers drink but why and how they drink it.

Arguably the most successful and effective spirits advertising campaign of all time was for Absolut Vodka. The now famous campaign centered on the vodka's unique bottle shape, and the ads' taglines played off the word *absolute*. One of the first ads featured a silkscreen painting of the brand's bottle by the artist Andy Warhol. Below the portrait were simply the words "Absolut Warhol." The ads were a major coup. Now it's hard to believe, but when it was first introduced, Absolut was virtually unknown, and the idea of a Scandinavian country producing quality vodka seemed very odd. The brand's medicinal bottle shape also was cause for concern because it was so different from the traditional, long-necked bottle design. Of course, the company's inventive advertising made Absolut extremely popular and synonymous with the word *vodka*. The trendy artists who designed many of the ads also lent the brand credibility and a downtown New York hipness. Absolut "made spirit advertising sexy," says Kenneth Hein, senior editor at *Brandweek* magazine. It also helped turn the bottle's shape from a liability into an asset. The success of Absolut helped launch the country's craze for vodka and started the modern era of premium spirits. The company "paved the way for the premium and super-premium explosion," says Hein.

Absolut's ads proved so popular, they were paid the ultimate compliment: many people ripped them out of magazines to save and hang like works of art. The ads were also collected into a coffee-table book and were exhibited in a museum and on a number of different websites. Ultimately, the campaign ran for 25 years and included over 1,500 different ads. It was so well respected that it earned the seventh spot on *Advertising Age* magazine's list of the 100 best ad campaigns of all time. (It came in behind such memorable campaigns as DeBeers's "A diamond is forever," and Nike's "Just do it.") Finally in 2006, Absolut reportedly invested $20 million to create a new campaign, which focused on the word *absolute* but abandoned using the spirit's signature bottle shape. For example, one of the new ads shows New York's Statue of Liberty, and the tag line reads "The Absolute Welcome." Many of the ads ran on television, a first for the brand.

Reportedly, the main reason for the switch in advertising was the success of the new generation of premium and super-premium vodkas. No brand has challenged Absolut's supremacy more than Grey Goose. In the late 1990s, master marketer Sidney Frank realized that many drinkers were ready and willing to spend more for vodka than the $15–$17 that Absolut cost. Frank priced his vodka at the then astronomical sum of $30 and justified the cost by insisting that his vodka was of a better quality. (Many consumers were willing to believe him based solely on the vodka's higher price tag.)

(continued)

But this was a lofty claim given the fact that vodka is supposed to be a neutral-tasting and neutral-smelling spirit. His proof? Grey Goose took top honors in a vodka competition held by the Chicago Beverage Testing Institute and won a platinum award at the World Spirits Competition in San Francisco. Afterwards Grey Goose began touting these results and began calling itself (and still does) "The World's Best Tasting Vodka."

This marketing strategy was a stroke of advertising genius on Frank's part. The campaign was simple but elegant. It answered the question that many consumers were asking: do more expensive spirits actually taste better than cheaper spirits? As a result of Grey Goose's ad, people felt smart and justified for buying the more expensive vodka. The claim, according to Hein, also allowed Frank to get bartenders on board who recommended the vodka to customers. No doubt they did so because it was also in their best interest. Bars could, of course, charge a premium for drinks if they were made with the pricier Grey Goose.

The ads might have impressed drinkers, but Frank's competitors were less than thrilled. Some of Grey Goose's original ads featured its top score from the Chicago Beverage Testing Institute as well as the scores of a number of its competitors. The Minnesota-based Millennium Import company, which imports the Polish premium Belvedere and Chopin vodkas, even sued Grey Goose and Sidney Frank Importing, alleging false advertising and libel. Millennium argued that the ads were incorrect because Belvedere scored much higher on subsequent taste tests. But the suit didn't stop Pravda Vodka from using a very similar ad with results from the World Beverage Championships in San Francisco, which judged the brand to be the best luxury vodka. Pravda's ad simply stated "Pravda Voted the Best Vodka."

Grey Goose's provocative ad campaign isn't the only recent spirits advertising controversy. Perhaps the biggest news was Seagram's 1996 television ads for Crown Royal Whisky and Lime Twisted Gin. Until then, the spirits brands had agreed to a ban on TV advertising. For decades, spirit companies spent most of their advertising budget on magazine ads and billboards. These didn't pose much competition for the beer companies, which were able to spend millions on catchy TV commercials and got a lot of consumers to shift from drinking spirits to beer. During the 1970s and 1980s, "we lost a lot of market share," admits Frank Coleman, senior vice president of the Distilled Spirits Council of the United States.

Seagram's commercials began a debate about whether or not the ban on spirits advertising should be lifted. Then in December 2001, Diageo, according to Hein, decided to take TV advertising to the next level. The spirits giant negotiated with NBC to buy time during the network's late-night programming. The first ad was for Smirnoff, and it ran during an episode of *Saturday Night Live.* The commercial created a firestorm of criticism. Ultimately the deal was canceled, but as a result of Diageo's aggressive move, spirit advertising has now become commonplace on cable TV stations and on local television channels. In 2001, the spirits industry, according to the Center on Alcohol Marketing and Youth (CAMY) at Georgetown University, spent $5 million on just under 2,000 cable ads. In 2005, that increased to almost 47,000 cable ads at a cost of $122 million. It's hard to calculate how much effect these ads had on increasing spirits sales, but no doubt they did help. (In fact, beer's market share is now decreasing.) Now the only question remains is when, not if, the networks will finally allow spirits ads back on prime time.

domed white-plastic container that looked as if it was a prop from the 1980s hit sci-fi movie *Tron*. Just like vodka makers, the ice cream companies boasted a range of flavors made with premium and exotic ingredients, like rum from Jamaica and chocolate from Ghana.

These pioneering high-end brands revolutionized the market for ice cream in America and paved the way for future innovators like Ben & Jerry. Mattus and his colleagues not only changed how the frozen dessert was made but also created the demand for it. Ever since, store freezer cases haven't been the same. No doubt premium vodkas have had the same effect upon the spirits industry. Now the only uncertainty for the category is how much consumers are willing to spend on a bottle.

CHAPTER 4 FOUR

Courtesy of Agua Luca

The Cocktail
Comeback

· · · · · · · ·

On Fridays, the rush begins after 5:00 PM, as workers unwind from another week penned up inside their cubicles and chained to their BlackBerries. By 9:00 PM, the rush is full-blown—all the tables are packed, and there's a crowd waiting around the bar. The staff valiantly tries to keep up with the flood of orders. Ingredients are quickly grabbed from the 20 reach-ins, which at the beginning of the night had been full of lemongrass, cucumbers, mint, and all kinds of fruit in wheels, slices, and twists. Servers fight through the crowds with loaded trays held high.

This hive of activity isn't some hot new celebrity-chef restaurant. In fact, this isn't a restaurant at all—it's a bar. Just a typical Friday night at New York City's Flatiron Lounge, which, in fact, serves no food but specializes in classic pre-Prohibition cocktails made with fresh ingredients. The art deco bar looks like an artifact from the city's past but actually dates to 2003. On a good weekend night, the Flatiron Lounge can serve up to 1,000 cocktails (not counting beer or wine), which cost around $12 each. For thirsty or adventurous patrons, the bar even serves a "flight of the day," three smaller cocktails based on a common theme. Reading the menu is like step-ping back in time. It lists long-forgotten cocktails, popular decades before most of the customers and bartenders were even born.

It would be easy to write off the Flatiron Lounge as some proto-typical New York City oddity. After all, you can find anything there if you look hard enough. But the success of the Flatiron Lounge is no fluke, and its appeal is certainly not limited to the five boroughs. The establishment is one of a new generation of cocktail bars that have opened across the country where drinks are mixed the old-fash-ioned way. And these bars aren't just packed with drink aficionados or octogenarians trying to relive their youth. People of all ages are ordering classic drinks like martinis, Manhattans, and Singapore slings as well as more exotic elixirs like mojitos and caipirinhas.

The past few years have been a golden age for cocktails. They're so popular that there's now a museum dedicated to mixed drinks: The Museum of the American Cocktail opened in the winter of 2005 in New Orleans's French Quarter. (After Hurricane Katrina, it had to temporarily relocate to New York and Las Vegas but will likely return to the Big Easy.) Cocktails are also pumping up the sales of spirits at bars and restaurants, which according to the Distilled Spir-its Council of the United States, were up 61 percent between 1997 and 2005. And even the food world has taken notice. *Food & Wine* magazine named 2006 the "Year of the Cocktail" and now publishes a guide to cocktails and bars. Dana Cowin, editor-in-chief of *Food & Wine*, told *USA Today*, "There is a definite diminution of food and an expansion of drinks."

At the forefront of this trend is a new breed of bartenders who call themselves "mixologists" or "bar chefs." To them, cocktails are an art. Their drinks are made with fresh ingredients and premium spirits, without shortcuts like sour mix. No detail is too small to be overlooked. Some mixologists, like Audrey Saunders of New York's Pegu Club, make their own ginger beer for drinks. The Double Seven, a swanky bar in New York's meatpacking district, uses three types of ice for different cocktails, including hand-cracked and chipped ice. "We think the ice is an important part of the cocktail and the taste of it," says Monika Chiang, the bar's managing partner and co-owner.

These expert bartenders aren't just dusting off old recipes. The last few years have also seen a boom for the creation of cocktail recipes. Bartenders are dreaming up new drinks and putting a modern spin on classics, adding popular ingredients like pomegranate, lychee, ginger, and even wasabi. The trend has helped wean customers off sugary apple martinis and cosmos. Bar chefs like Scott Beattie of the restaurant Cyrus in Healdsburg, California, are using fresh seasonal herbs, spices, fruits, and even vegetables to flavor their drinks. Beattie buys many of his ingredients from local farmers and even grows some of them himself. Now the cocktail menus of upscale bars and restaurants—like food menus—often change depending upon the season and the availability of fruits and vegetables. Some of these menus are more like small books. At Cyrus, Beattie offers patrons a 45-page cocktail and spirits menu, which gives detailed descriptions of each spirit served at the bar.

But this isn't the first cocktail boom. The cocktail actually has a very long history. Even though it's an American invention, according to David Wondrich, cocktail historian and *Esquire* magazine's drink correspondent, "The cocktail has deep roots in England." People were drinking medicinal cocktails made with bitters, usually a mixture of alcohol and herbs, across the pond as early as the 1700s to cure their punch or brandy-induced hangovers. The first use of the word *cocktail* in print appeared in an 1803 newspaper in Amherst, New Hampshire. According to Wondrich, the term was used in a satirical story about the life of a so-called "lounger." And the earliest definition for *cocktail* that anyone has found was printed in the Hudson, New York, newspaper *The Balance and Columbian Repository* in 1806. The paper gave its readers this definition: "Cock tail, then, is a stimulating liquor, composed of spirits of any kind, sugar, water and bitters. It is vulgarly called a bittered sling . . . ." The editor provided the definition in response to a reader's inquiry because a previous story had mentioned a "Cock Tail." The primary difference between a proper cocktail and the other drinks that people made at the time was bitters. Unfortunately, the article doesn't give any information on the origin of the word, and no one has been able to determine the derivation of the term or who coined it. There are, of course, several competing theories.

No matter where the name originated, by the 1830s, the bar culture and the popularity of cocktails began to take off. Unlike Europeans, who preferred wine and brandy, the early Americans were already fans of hard spirits, usually homegrown rye and corn-based whiskey. This preference was born, for the most part, out of necessity. Most Americans couldn't afford alcohol imported from Europe, and after breaking with the British Empire, the supply of rum and molasses from the Caribbean was severely limited. These early homegrown spirits could be rough, and cocktails provided a way to even out or mask their harsh taste.

The increasing availability of ice also popularized cocktails. Frederic Tudor built an empire on the innovative idea that you could harvest ice from frozen lakes or ponds and then ship it all over the world. The sherry cobbler and the mint julep were the first two cocktails to use ice. By the 1850s, the novelty of ice had worn off, and people expected their cocktails to be served cold.

In the late 1840s, James W. Marshall discovered gold while working on the construction of Sutter's Mill in what is today Coloma, California. This discovery set off the California Gold Rush and ushered in a period of wealth and prosperity. "America was getting rich, and people were looking for luxury," says Wondrich. Instead of just local whiskey, bars were soon offering imported spirits, including Dutch gin, French brandy, and champagne. Even in the gold-mining camps, you could order a fancy champagne cocktail. "Miners were getting rich and wanted to blow their money," Wondrich says.

But fancy cocktails weren't only being served in small mining towns. In 1853, the lavish Bank Exchange saloon opened in San Francisco, complete with marble floors, expensive oil paintings, and a long mahogany bar. Nine years later, Jerry Thomas, a celebrity bartender who had run bars across the country and was said to have had a solid silver bar set, published the first cocktail cookbook aptly called *How to Mix Drinks or The Bon Vivant's Companion.* The seminal volume is still required reading for serious mixologists, and vintage copies are rare and expensive. (Fortunately, in early 2004, the book was reissued and is again in print and widely available.) Still, until about 1870, most cocktails were made with just alcohol, sugar, and bitters.

But bartenders soon began using other ingredients, such as fresh juices and vermouth, to expand their repertoire of drinks. Until that point, according to Wondrich, juices were only used in punches but not cocktails. This gave rise to one of the most innovative and productive periods in the history of the cocktail, when many of the classic drinks were created, including the martini, the Manhattan, and the daiquiri. It's no wonder that master mixologist Dale DeGroff calls the 1870s "the height of the cocktail's golden age" in his book *The Craft of the Cocktail.* And according to Stephen Visakay, cocktail shaker collector and author of the book *Vintage Bar Ware,* this was also an innovative period for bartending tools. Before the American Civil War, bartenders would mix drinks by pouring the ingredients back and forth between two cups. After the Civil War, most bartenders began using a two-piece cocktail shaker. It was developed when an innkeeper found that he could connect the two glasses with a little pressure. (This now-ubiquitous shaker is often referred to as a Boston Shaker and is made from a pint glass and a slightly larger metal cup.) The shaker allowed the bartender to mix the ingredients

together thoroughly and create a cold, frothy drink. Also, it also gave
the cocktail "a little more kinetic energy," says Wondrich. The better
bars, according to DeGroff, had soda water and were equipped with
beer taps and even early refrigerators.

But this historic period was short-lived. By the 1920s, the golden
age of cocktails was coming to an end, with Prohibition and the
Great Depression looming. As speakeasies replaced fancy saloons,
the quality of the cocktails suffered. Bartending had been a noble
profession, requiring a two-year apprenticeship, but during Prohibition, the job took on a seedy connotation that it would not shake
for decades. People began treating bartending "as a vocation and not
an occupation," says Kim Haasarud, founder of drink consultancy
Liquid Architecture and author of *101 Martinis.* "It took only 10 or
15 years to destroy a thriving industry."

Bars and bartenders bore the brunt of Prohibition, but that
didn't mean people stopped drinking cocktails. Illegal underground
bars opened around the country, and "Prohibition was a boom for
people mixing drinks at home," says Wondrich. "Before that it was
a professional's job." Cocktails were particularly popular because
illicitly brewed spirits often tasted harsh if consumed straight. As
a result, stores were flooded with cocktail shakers. According to
Visakay, the golden age for cocktail shakers started in 1920 and
continued until just before the United States entered World War II.
During the Jazz Age, shakers looked like tea pots and were angular
with sharp edges. For high rollers, there were also fancy sterling
silver novelty shakers made in the late 1920s, including some in the
shape of golf bags and lighthouses. But after the 1929 stock market
crash, fancy shakers were replaced by less expensive streamlined
and skyscraper-like glass and chrome models. "Every family had
a cocktail shaker on their shelf," says Visakay. Top art deco indus-
trial designers, including Norman Bel Geddes and Russel Wright,
designed cocktail sets making use of popular materials, like chrome

and Bakelite. The futuristic style was designed to uplift people from the throes of the Depression and to give them hope for a better and exciting future.

During World War II, the production of cocktail shakers was suspended because the materials were needed for the war effort. Once the war ended, the formerly vibrant cocktail culture had a hard time rebounding. Even though the 1950s is often symbolized by a man in the gray flannel suit drinking a super-dry martini, the decade was in reality a low point for cocktails. America had entered the Atomic Age, and in the quest to become more high-tech, shakers were replaced by blenders, and fresh ingredients were replaced by artificially flavored drink mixes. As a result, many of the classic cocktails faded from menus and from the collective conscience. Even rye whiskey began to disappear from bar shelves. In the decade's quest to modernize and streamline, many traditions were left behind. Unfortunately traditional cocktails were among them.

Fortunately, there were a few exceptions: "The two great things you could drink in the '50s were a dry martini or a Tiki drink," says Wondrich. The Tiki culture, led by Victor "Trader Vic" Bergeron and his signature mai tai cocktail, was a definite highlight of the postwar period. According to Bergeron, he invented the rum based drink in 1944 while working at his Oakland, California, restaurant. In an account that he wrote in 1970 defending his claim as the father of the mai tai, Trader Vic explained that he was inspired by a 17- year-old bottle of Wray & Nephew Jamaican rum that he had on his shelf. He called the drink a mai tai because he served the concoction to two Tahitian friends who supposedly exclaimed "mai tai—roe ae," which means "Out of this world—the best." The rest is history. Bergeron introduced the drink to the world through his chain of Trader Vic's restaurants, which are still operating and expanding. The chain expects to open locations in Jordan and Beijing in 2007.

Trader Vic: The Father of the Mai Tai
The tiki trendsetter

The birth place of the mai tai, the classic tiki cocktail, wasn't Hawaii or Polynesia, but, of all places, Oakland, California. And its inventor was a garrulous, one-legged bartender named Victor Bergeron. (The closest he came to having exotic origins was having a French-Canadian father.) Thanks to his cocktail recipes and his love of the faux Polynesian lifestyle, Bergeron became famous around the world as "Trader Vic." His single California restaurant spawned a chain that's still opening new locations today.

It all started with the Hinky Dink's restaurant he opened in 1934. It was definitely a family affair. An aunt loaned him $800, and his wife's brother helped Bergeron renovate the space. The restaurant soon evolved into Trader Vic's, serving what his company now calls "Island-Eurasian Cuisine." At the time, this fusion style was revolutionary, and it soon became very popular. But most important was the mai tai, which Trader Vic invented in 1944.

In 1951, he introduced the cocktail to Hawaii, where it was naturally a big hit. In 1955, he opened a second Trader Vic's in Beverly Hills, California. Throughout the 1950s and 1960s, Trader Vic's began popping up all over the country and around the world, including locations in London, Cuba, Munich, and Osaka. In addition to offering an excellent selection of cocktails, Bergeron, an early fan of the budding California wine industry, put the region's wines on his menus. He also started a successful line of packaged foods and cocktail supplies, not to mention a second chain of Señor Pico Mexican restaurants. The first location opened in San Francisco in 1964. (Today there are only two Señor Pico restaurants left—oddly one is in Muscat, Oman, and the other is in Bangkok, Thailand.)

The Trader passed away in 1984, leaving the restaurant chain in the hands of his family, and the company has continued to prosper. In fact, the company-owned and franchise-owned restaurants collectively earn about $70 million a year. The company has expanded to the Middle East and Asia, and thanks to the new popularity of cocktails, on some United Airlines flights you can enjoy the Trader's food and mai tai cocktails.

What helped tiki bars and culture catch on was a fascination with Hawaii, which became America's 50th state in 1959. The trend was also encouraged by the film *South Pacific* (1958) and the 1961 Elvis vehicle *Blue Hawaii*. According to the website of the London tiki bar Trailer Happiness, the tiki heyday was between 1955 and 1965, and "tiki drinks and dining injected new hope and optimism into a postwar, cold-war society."

But over the next couple of decades, classic cocktails were mostly forgotten. Sure, an occasional martini or a gimlet was ordered, but most Americans drank beer, whisky, or simple mixed drinks, like rum and Coke or gin and tonic. And when someone ordered a proper cocktail, most likely the bartender used shortcuts like mixes or canned juices. "People really got away from fresh, and it never recovered," says Julie Reiner, co-owner of the Flatiron Lounge and the Pegu Club. To young people in the 1960s and 1970s, cocktails seemed like their parents' and grandparents' drinks, thoroughly uncool and antiquated.

Change came in the mid-1980s. The country began an obsession with white spirits, specifically Absolut vodka, introduced to the United States in 1979. These spirits were easily mixed with juices and other ingredients and provided an introduction to cocktails for people who hadn't grown up drinking them.

A watershed moment occurred in late 1980s when Joe Baum, the former head of Restaurant Associates, was hired to renovate New York's historic Rainbow Room restaurant (complete with a revolving dance floor), located on the 65th floor of 30 Rockefeller Plaza. For years, Baum was a driving force behind the New York restaurant scene, and he created such institutions as The Four Seasons restaurant, the Forum of the Twelve Caesars, and Windows on the World. The reportedly $25 million makeover of the Rainbow Room wasn't just about raising floors to get better views, which he did, but about conjuring an air of sophistication and luxury.

Dale DeGroff heard about the plans for the Rainbow Room while running the bar at Aurora, another of Baum's restaurants. He came up with the idea for a bar at the Rainbow Room that would offer drinks that had been served in all the famous New York supper clubs. DeGroff believed that a bar serving classic cocktails made with fresh juices and without any shortcuts would set the restaurant apart from just about every other establishment in the city; the bar would help give the Rainbow Room a feeling of elegance. Baum liked the idea and requested a potential drinks menu. Even though DeGroff had been making cocktails the old-fashioned way at Aurora (at Baum's request), he scrambled to locate old recipes and was able to borrow some vintage cocktail books from a drinks enthusiast.

Fortunately for the future of the cocktail, DeGroff excelled at shaking and developing drinks. The Rainbow Room became a grand stage for DeGroff to show off his cocktails. "It was Joe's crowning achievement," DeGroff says. "The Rainbow Room was his dream."

In addition to resurrecting and popularizing numerous drinks that seemed destined to be forgotten, DeGroff was also an innovator. In February 1995, he orchestrated the first of three cocktail dinners at the Rainbow Room. The dinner was unlike any meal in modern history. DeGroff paired each course of the special menu with a different cocktail. "I did it on a lark," he admits. The idea came to him at about 2:30 one morning while he was enjoying a postwork snack at Blue Ribbon downtown. He was drinking a glass of smoky Lagavulin Scottish whisky when his Thai fish soup arrived. The whisky went so well with the soup that he had a sudden epiphany: pairing food with cocktails instead of wine. "Gee, what a cool idea," he thought to himself. The first dinner was a success and effectively served notice that cocktails were back and should be treated seriously. Since then, these cocktail dinners have become one of DeGroff's signatures. In 2006, he held one every month at the Commander's Palace in Las Vegas.

Ultimately DeGroff ran the Rainbow Room's bar for 12 years until the restaurant was taken over by the Cipriani family, the famed owners of Harry's Bar in Venice, Italy. He continues to be a driving force in the cocktail industry, training bartenders around the country and consulting on numerous cocktail lists. (To find out more about DeGroff, read the profile of him in this chapter.) His legacy in the cocktail industry is immeasurable. Many enthusiasts and experts point to DeGroff's appointment at the Rainbow Room as the key force behind the resurgence of the cocktail.

DeGroff's timing was perfect. "Different trends rub together and catch a spark," says Wondrich. With "no cultural moment, he would have just continued to make good drinks." One such trend was a sudden nostalgia for retro music and culture, including cabaret singers and Gershwin tunes. In the late 1980s, a young singer from New Orleans named Harry Connick, Jr. burst onto the music scene, singing torch songs that hadn't been popular in decades. In 1989, he crooned the classics for the soundtrack of the smash hit movie *When Harry Met Sally.* A few years later, Natalie Cole's album *Unforgettable,* featuring a duet with her late father Nat King Cole, won the Grammy award for record of year as well as the Grammy award for album of the year. Even swing dancing became fashionable again. The 1996 movie *Swingers* immortalized

Dale DeGroff: Master Mixologist
The father of the cocktail renaissance

It's hard to find a high-end cocktail bar that hasn't been influenced in some way by Dale DeGroff, whether he's designed the drinks menu, contributed a recipe, or trained the bar staff. DeGroff has become the consummate bartender's bartender and the authority on cocktail recipes and history. He's the first source called by spirits writers, beverage directors, and liquor companies. If you're lucky enough to sit at a bar he's tending, he'll fill your glass with one tasty elixir after another, and like any good bartender, he'll regale you with one entertaining story after another. But perhaps his most interesting story is his own.

DeGroff, the son of a navy pilot, grew up all over the world. As a teenager, he lived in Spain, Morocco, and then Rhode Island. But after seeing *West Side Story* as a kid, it became his lifelong dream to live in New York City. He moved there in 1969 to pursue an acting career. To make money, he began working at an ad agency that had Restaurant Associates as a client. Thanks to this connection, DeGroff frequently ate in the company's many restaurants, including The Four Seasons, the Forum of the Twelve Caesars, and La Fonda del Sol. As a result, "I had this early education in food and especially drink," he says. And he got to experience the "the old-fashioned bar life."

Before long, DeGroff started working at restaurants—but not behind the bar. DeGroff started as a dishwasher at the Howard Johnson in Times Square. He then worked as a waiter in Charley O's. There came the turning point in DeGroff's life (and arguably the future success of the cocktail). One morning, he had just finished packing a truck of provisions for a party that Charley O's was catering at New York's Gracie Mansion (the mayor's traditional home). The bartender who was supposed to work the party didn't show up. DeGroff heard the commotion and, on the spur of the moment, volunteered. "I lied and said I was a bartender," he says. After getting a scribbled cocktail recipe crib sheet, he headed uptown to the party. The gig turned out to be relatively easy, but there was something about being behind the bar that he really enjoyed.

In 1978, DeGroff and his wife, Jill, moved to Los Angeles to give acting another chance. Like most actors starting out, he also needed a day job. On his second day in L.A., he got a job at the ritzy Hotel Bel-Air as a bartender. The bar had a loyal and often celebrity clientele. On his days off, he worked at bars all over town, including the Magic Castle and the Variety Arts Club. Most of these bars used sour mix and canned juices, but DeGroff quickly realized that the tips were bigger if he hand-squeezed the limes.

By 1985, he was back in New York running the bar at Aurora. The midtown restaurant was owned by Joe Baum, the former head of Restaurant Associates. When it opened, "it was considered the apogee of French-American sophistication, the Versailles in Joe Baum's impressive collection of culinary chateaus," wrote Bryan Miller, the New York Times restaurant critic in a 1989 review. But unlike the owners of the other bars where DeGroff worked, Baum wanted cocktails to be made the old-fashioned way with fresh juices and without mixes or shortcuts. It was a daunting task, but Baum was determined to have it his way, and he made sure that every drink met his exacting standards. DeGroff was forced to track down old cocktail books to relearn this lost art. Working at Aurora was a great education for him, even if it was painful at times. In his book The Craft of the Cocktail, DeGroff describes what it was like

(continued)

working for Baum: "When considering drinks to put on his menu, Joe would order the same drink three times in a row and then move on to another drink until he tasted one that pleased him. It wasn't an easy process—then again nothing was easy with Joe. When he didn't like a drink, there was no explanation: it was simply wrong and needed fixing. I would taste it and try to improve it."

DeGroff lobbied Baum to hire him for his new project: the renovated Rainbow Room. DeGroff ran the legendary restaurant's Promenade Bar for 12 years, helping to expose thousands of people to classically made drinks and training many bartenders. His work at the Rainbow Room kick-started the rebirth of the cocktail. He left the restaurant after the lease for the Rainbow Room was taken over by the Cipriani family. Since then, the "King of Cocktails," as DeGroff has come to be known, has trained countless bartenders and designed numerous cocktail menus around the world. He and his wife were among the primary founders of the Museum of the American Cocktail, which now offers exhibitions and seminars in New York and Las Vegas. And as the dean of bartending, DeGroff continues to add to his legacy, ensuring the popularity and enjoyment of well-mixed cocktails.

the retro movement in Los Angeles and instantly made zoot suits, cabana lounge wear, big band swing music, and, most important, cocktails very cool. Much of the film follows a group of hipsters as they go from one cozy old-school L.A. bar to another. The movie's poster features a young Vince Vaughn toasting the camera with a martini glass. The title is emblazoned across a bar matchbook with the tag line "Get a nightlife." There couldn't have been a better advertisement for cocktails.

George Washington was one of the country's first commercial distillers. His distillery at Mount Vernon was recently reconstructed.

Cognac is aged for years in dark, cool and dusty warehouses. This is one of Otard's many casks.

Absolut Vodka jump-started the current spirits craze with its series of clever ads, including this one titled Absolut LA. The ads were so popular that they became collectibles.

(right) Sidney Frank bottled his French vodka in an impressive and eye-catching bottle to ensure that consumers realized it was a luxury brand. *(far right)* In 2000, Diageo introduced the first super-premium gin Tanqueray No. Ten in this iconic statuesque bottle.

The Strathisla Distillery is the home of the Scottish Chivas Regal. Most of the single malt it produces goes into the different Chivas blends.

The Macallan Fine and Rare Collection launched in 2002 with 10,000 bottles of 37 distinctive vintages covering more than 116 years valued at the time at $20 million.

Up in the Scottish highlands these hard working stills make The Glenlivet.

This is the Glennfiddich still house, which produces the number one single malt whisky in the world.

Glennfiddich is one of the few Scottish distilleries to still run its own cooperage.

Up until a few years ago Macallan only produced whisky aged in sherry oak wood, like this 18 year old.

This streamlined cocktail set was designed by Norman Bel Geddes and made by the Revere Copper & Brass Company between 1935 and 1940. It has become a favorite of collectors.

This silver-plated cocktail shaker with red plastic accents was made in the late 1920s.

The Scandinavian restaurant Aquavit is one of the first establishments to bottle its own spirit. Aquavit New York is made in Sweden and flavored with Massachusetts white cranberries.

Contrary to popular belief tequila is not made from cactus but from agave, a member of the lily family. This is one of Tequila Don Julio's *jimadores* harvesting an agave plant.

Tequila Don Julio's warehouse and bottling plant.

Another factor that helped spark the sudden interest in cocktails was a traveling exhibit of the top 100 cocktail shakers from Stephen Visakay's renowned collection. The shakers were made between 1904 and 1950, covering the full range of shaker production. The exhibit toured from 1993 to 1998 and was displayed in seven American and Canadian museums, including the Milwaukee Art Museum and The Louisiana State Museum. The exhibit and the renewed interest in drinking cocktails spurred a collecting craze for antique shakers and barware. In the spring of 1997, Visakay published a catalog for the traveling show called *Vintage Bar Ware,* still considered the definitive book on the subject. (Ads online for barware often site specific page numbers from Visakay's book.) When he started collecting shakers in the late 1970s, before eBay and the Internet, he could find them relatively easily at flea markets and antique stores, often for little money. (The one exception were designer art deco shakers from the 1930s, which were always sought after and never cheap.)

By the late 1990s, prices increased dramatically as shakers became increasingly more popular, viewed as legitimate antiques and investments. Unfortunately, the competition made it increasingly difficult for collectors to add new shakers to their collections. "It was over for me," says Visakay, who hasn't bought a shaker in more than six years. The shakers became so valuable that he decided to sell off part of his own collection, which had grown to include over 1,600 items. In June 2001, Philips auctioned off 20 of Visakay's top cocktail shakers. After the last gavel fell, the auction totaled just under $250,000 (including the buyer's commission to the house), triple the preauction estimate. One silver shaker, an 18-inch cross between an airplane and a zeppelin, went for an astonishing $52,000. A Russel Wright shaker that Visakay had bought for $600 at a New York City antique show went for $6,000.

Mixology for Dummies
A small New England company makes mixing cocktails easy.

Muddling, shaking, and straining are a lot of hard work, but you can whip up fancy cocktails, like mojitos, peach bellinis, and mango margaritas, without breaking a sweat or even squeezing a lime. An increasing number of people are letting a small New England company called Stirrings do the hard work for them. You can use one of the company's 18 high-end cocktail mixes to whip up a tasty elixir. Best of all, you won't be ashamed of letting your guests see the bottle.

Since the 1950s, many bottled cocktail mixers and shortcuts have been on store shelves, including mixes from Mr. & Mrs. T and the restaurant chain T.G.I. Friday's. But what sets Stirrings products apart is that they're made with natural juices, triple-purified water, and cane sugar and are packaged in hip designer containers. The products are also sold in high-end stores like Williams-Sonoma, Sur La Table, Gourmet Garage, and Whole Foods. And now you can even enjoy a Stirrings cocktail in the air. In 2006, Delta partnered with the company to offer drinks in their clubs and on flights.

Surprisingly, Stirrings was only started in 1997 by two best friends whose experience in the spirits industry was limited to bartending during college. The partners first began by producing high-end rubs, salts, and spices for cooking under the name Nantucket Off-Shore. One day, it occurred to them to try some of their high-end Fleur de Sel on the rim of a margarita glass. At the time, many restaurants were making the cocktail with expensive tequila and fresh ingredients but were ruining the drink by using harsh, cheap salt. The high-quality imported salt was a huge improvement. The next step was trying to flavor the salt with lime or cilantro to better complement the cocktail. Naturally the first Stirrings products were high-end salts for drinks. The company has since introduced a number of different drink-related products, including cocktail mixes, simple syrup, and bitters. Stirrings also has a line of highly carbonated tonic water, club soda, and ginger ale, which should stay bubbly longer.

But the company's products weren't an immediate hit. It took some time to convince store owners that people would spend $8.99 or $9.99 on a Stirrings mix instead of $2.99 to $4.99, the price of most mixes. "Everyone thought we were crazy," says the company's cofounder, Gil MacLean. "We had a lot of pushback and had to create the market for the product." But the Stirrings products turned out to be very popular. One reason was the sudden interest in premium spirits. Because people were spending $30 or more for a bottle of vodka or gin, they wanted a premium mixer. The company's mixes have also been a hit with bartenders and restaurant owners. "We had a huge amount of success because we were filling a huge niche and redefining cocktail mixes," says MacLean.

How successful has the company become? In 2005, Stirrings had revenues of $13.6 million, up almost 1,000 percent over the last three years. The performance was good enough to garner a spot on *Inc.* magazine's list of 500 fastest-growing private companies in 2006. Sales have been so strong, the company moved into a new facility in Fall River, Massachusetts, complete with decorative Meyer lemon trees, gym, café, and, most importantly, an extra big bar.

Today several websites and stores across the country, not to mention eBay, offer big selections of vintage barware. A recent search of eBay using the search term "cocktail shaker" yielded 468 lots.

Another result of Visakay's show and the sudden popularity of vintage barware was that all types of stores began selling cocktail shakers, including Restoration Hardware, which stocked retro penguin and zeppelin models. And just as shakers were designed by famous designers like Bel Geddes and Wright in the 1920s, today the hip Italian housewares design company, Alessi, offers a number of shakers. But you don't have to spend a lot on a designer shaker. Michael Graves designed a bar set for Target that included a strainer, bar knife, jigger, bottle opener, and ice scoop, which sold for just $25.

The cocktail also got help from an unlikely place: the kitchen. The 1990s could be called the Food Decade, when cooking becoming a national passion that turned chefs into bona fide celebrities and restaurants into significant cultural institutions. One big reason was the 1993 launch of the Food Network, which now reaches 90 million homes in the United States alone. Suddenly people cared about the food they were eating, where it came from, and how it was grown. By 1999, the upscale purveyor of sustainably grown groceries, Whole Foods Market, opened its 100th store in Torrance, California. In just 20 years, Whole Foods went from a single store in progressive Austin, Texas, to a mainstream national chain popular both with aging, patchouli-scented hippies and SUV-driving soccer moms.

Bars and liquor stores weren't immune to the trend. The market for wine, specifically California wine, took off in the '90s. As people began to learn more about wine and develop their palates, they began to buy not only mass-produced Kendall-Jackson but also expensive bottles. The first vintages from Opus One, the joint venture between Robert Mondavi and Baron Philippe de Rothschild, were released in 1984. By 1995, a single bottle of the original vintage of Opus One sold for $250 at auction. That seems like a bargain compared to the prices that small, upstart cult wines soon garnered. At auction or on wine lists, a bottle of Screaming Eagle, one of the best-known boutique wineries, was soon selling for a $1,000 or more. Thanks to small yields, high scores from critic Robert Parker, and intense media coverage, these wines became increasingly hard to buy even if you had the cash. Many of the top wineries would only sell wine to people on their mailing lists, which meant a whole season's supply would be sold out months in advance.

This new interest in food and wine connoisseurship lead many people to rediscover spirits, especially the boutique spirits that began to appear on shelves. Some of the earliest were produced by Fritz Maytag of San Francisco's famed Anchor Steam Beer. In 1993, he founded Anchor Distilling, which according to the company's website "is dedicated to creating very small batches of traditionally distilled spirits of many types and styles." The company now offers a range of interesting whiskies and a gin. People also began drinking ever more expensive spirits, in particular high-end vodka. Some drinkers also began to taste, sniff, and even sometimes spit spirits as if they were wines. Suddenly people were ordering their mixed drinks made with premium spirits, even if it cost more. "People's palates have changed," says Chiang of New York's The Double Seven. "People have become more sophisticated in their drinking."

Soon, fancy bars and lounges sprouted up in New York, offering classically made cocktails without any shortcuts. "This was really an untapped market," says Julie Reiner, who co-owns two bars in the city. "New Yorkers will travel for good food and will travel for really good drinks." And it wasn't just their cocktail menus that harkened back to an earlier time. Many of these establishments looked as if they were movie sets, from art deco lounges to postcolonial officer's clubs somewhere in the jungles of Southeast Asia. One of the first to open was the clublike Bar and Books in 1990, which offered cocktails as well as cigars. The bar grew to include two locations in New York and a third in Prague.

On the West Coast, especially in San Francisco, a number of bars began using fresh juices for their cocktail recipes. This boom was greeted gratefully by cocktail fans and kindly by the press. It was appealing to bar owners as well, because the potential profits were great. "Frankly, that's where the money is," says Mark Grossich, CEO of Hospitality Holdings, which owns a number of high-end bars in New York. (He also was one of the original owners of Bar and Books.) Because many restaurants only break even on food and make their profits on their beverage service, Grossich figured, why bother serving food at all? And it seems he was right. At Hospitality Holdings' establishments, the average check pushes $50. At the Campbell Apartment, tucked into a corner of New York's Grand Central Station, which Grossich opened in 1999, it's easy to understand how a bill gets so bloated, since the best-selling cocktail is the $15 Prohibition punch. The pricy cocktail is a perfect match for the opulent private-club feel of the bar.

Just as cocktails regularly appeared in the movies during their heyday, mixed drinks began showing up again on the big and small screens. The 1930s had the *Thin Man* movies with Nick and Nora mixing up martinis. The 1990s had Carrie Bradshaw and her friends downing cosmos and dirty martinis across New York City. The TV show, *Sex and the City*, which debuted on HBO in 1998 and ran for six seasons, made Sarah Jessica Parker and her costars huge celebrities. Almost every episode included at least one scene of the women rehashing the previous night's dates over brunch and a scene where they were out at some hip lounge, bar, or restaurant, cocktails in hand. Practically overnight, as the show's viewers became loyal to the point of obsession, the popularity of cosmos and other cocktails ordered by Parker and her costars reached new highs. The show "definitely helped," says Reiner. It "created a heightened awareness." It also dispelled any notion that cocktails were just for men. Drinks became so synonymous with the series,

Cocktail Menu

Not that long ago, the only place where you could find a "Bronx," a "sidecar" or an "aviation" was a dusty cocktail cookbook. But over the last decade around the world, there has been a rebirth of high-end cocktail bars that use fresh ingredients and traditional techniques to produce cocktail classics in all their glory. For the self-styled mixologists and bar chefs employed in these bars, perfection is in the details, from extra-large ice cubes to homemade ginger beer. But expect to pay a premium for these elixirs. Some of these bars charge $16 per drink. Here's a list of some of the best cocktail bars, which are definitely worth visiting. (Just don't order a rum and Coke.)

New York

- *Pegu Club (77 West Houston Street).* If you're not careful, you'll miss the entrance to the Pegu Club. Those who find it are transported back in time and across continents. The second-floor, swanky bar/lounge has the exotic and welcoming feel of an expat hangout somewhere in the Far East. After all, it is named for a British officer's club in Burma. The cocktail menu is only a few pages long but is packed with delicious drinks made with fresh and interesting ingredients.

- *Flatiron Lounge (37 West 19th Street).* This art deco monument to cocktails is located in New York's Flatiron District. Open since the spring of 2003, its cocktail menu changes frequently and features drinks made by guest celebrity mixologists. Be sure to try the "flight of the day," composed of three small drinks with a common theme or flavor.

(continued)

- *Campbell Apartment (15 Vanderbilt Avenue).* Finding a well-mixed cocktail in Grand Central Station used to be a real challenge, but now just outside the Vanderbilt Avenue entrance, the Campbell Apartment is housed in the ornate former office of 1920's business tycoon John W. Campbell. The bar is a perfect spot for an after-work cocktail. Unfortunately, you won't be admitted wearing sneakers or jeans.

- *Employees Only (510 Hudson Street).* Guarding the door of this Greenwich Village restaurant and bar is a burly doorman and a fortune teller who will gladly read your palm or tarot cards. Push past the psychic (she won't be offended; she was expecting it) through the heavy curtains, and you'll find yourself in one of New York's hippest establishments. The bartenders even wear traditional, short white jackets. They whip up excellent drinks, including a Pimm's cup, Hemingway daiquiri, and a West Side. The bar's low profile attracts a loyal following of hip young New Yorkers.

London

- *Salvatore at Fifty (50 St. James Street).* Do whatever you can to get into London's private club Fifty. The club opened in 1827 and was recently remodeled. One of the new additions is the luxurious bar, Salvatore at Fifty, named for and run by one of Britain's most famous bartenders, Salvatore Calabrese. In addition to a long list of innovative cocktails, the bar stocks a fine collection of vintage cognac.

- *Match Bar (37–38 Margaret Street).* The rebirth of the cocktail has been led by drinkers in two cities: New York and London. And across the Pond, it's getting almost as easy to find a well-mixed drink as a well-poured pint. One reason is the chain of three hip

Match bars located across London, which serve classic cocktails as well as a full food menu.

- *Trailer Happiness (177 Portobello Road)*. In the trendy London neighborhood of Notting Hill, immortalized by the Hugh Grant and Julia Roberts movie, is a shrine to the bygone tiki bar called Trailer Happiness. The bar bills itself as "a retro-sexual haven of cosmopolitan kitsch and faded trailer park glamour." And the drinks menu doesn't disappoint. It includes such tiki classics as zombies, mai tais, and scorpion bowls.

Prague

- *Bar and Books (Tynska 19)*. Just steps from the scenic Charles Bridge and off one of Prague's famous winding, Kafkaesque streets is the dark and comfy Bar and Books. In addition to well-mixed drinks, the establishment also offers a fine selection of cigars. The original Bar and Books is located in New York City, but the one in Prague is not to be missed, especially since the exchange rate makes the drinks a bargain.

HBO's website sold a martini glass, perfect for a cosmo, with the show's logo. For a time, it was hard to find a bar that wasn't offering a cosmo or some other martini variation. Anything served in a martini glass was awarded the *tini* suffix, no matter how untraditional the recipe. Bars were soon handing patrons phonebook-sized martini menus, with dozens of drinks that were made with all kinds of exotic ingredients, including chocolate, sour apple, and even butterscotch schnapps.

By the turn of the century, the popularity of cocktails was well established, so much so that in April 2002, the *New York Times* started running a column in the Sunday "Styles" section on cocktails called "Shaken and Stirred." And when *The Wall Street Journal* started its weekend paper, *Pursuits,* in September 2005, it included a weekly column on cocktails and spirits in addition to the paper's wine coverage. Even airlines are again serving cocktails in an attempt to regain an aura of sophistication and luxury that travel has lost over the years. In 2006, Delta Air Lines announced that it would begin serving a line of specialty cocktails on all domestic flights and in its airport clubs. The airline's first signature cocktail was the "mile-high mojito," which cost passengers $5. Delta still uses a mix, but at least it's made by Stirrings from real juice and natural ingredients. Not to be outdone, United announced a few months later that it had partnered with Trader Vic's to serve his famous mai tais and Polynesian food on select flights.

You can find a great pre-Prohibition cocktail at many hotel bars. Hotel companies realized that guests were leaving the property to drink at fancy bars and lounges. By redoing the bars and introducing upscale cocktails, hotel managers could keep guests inside the hotel buying drinks. Some hotels have been so successful that their bars now attract not just guests but locals. There's a "huge revenue upside," says Matthew Von Ertfelda, vice president of restaurants and bars at Marriott. At some of his company's hotels, revenue has doubled when bars and cocktail menus have been redone. There's "a lot of money to be made in mixology today," he says. In fact, Marriott recently launched its Bar Arts program, which calls for premium spirits and fresh juices at all Marriott and Renaissance bars in the United States. Working with Dale DeGroff, the company has put together a book of 150 cocktail recipes (with images) from which each bar hotel can choose. But "a lot of properties freak out when you say fresh juice," says Von Ertfelda. It's understandable, since even though fresh ingredients make better drinks, they are expensive and can be labor-intensive to prepare. It's obviously easier to just open a can of juice than to squeeze a crate of oranges. To make the transition a little easier, the company is also bringing in different mixologists to help train the hotel's bartenders.

Some luxury hotels have gone even further. The Sky View Bar in the Burj Al Arab hotel in Dubai, offers custom cocktails made tableside. The bar has a mixology cart run by two bartenders who will come up with a unique drink for you based on your personal preferences. The guest even gets to name the concoction and gets a copy of the recipe. And because the bar comes to you, the guest gets a close view of the bartender in action. But you can find a luxury hotel bar a lot closer than Dubai. The Dorchester in London hired celebrity architect and interior designer Thierry Despont to redo the hotel's bar. After the renovation, the bar's opening was such a big event that it was attended by celebrities, including Kate Moss and Jade Jagger. The new bar design features lacquered mahogany walls, plush velvet banquets, and decorative red glass, spearlike sculptures. And it's not just about the bar anymore. The Fairmont Hotel chain has introduced ten signature cocktails and an accompanying CD of lounge music with songs from Diana Krall, Mel Torme, and Rosemary Clooney. Guests can sip classic cocktails and listen to classic lounge tunes. When they check out, they can purchase the CD to listen to when they mix drinks at home.

Well-mixed cocktails are also now available on the high seas. Bars on cruise ships are famous for serving bottomless cups of fruity blender cocktails like piña coladas and frozen margaritas. Holland America Line is trying to change this reputation. The cruise company has consulted with a number of well-known mixologists to give the bars on all five of its ships a makeover. Each day, bartenders squeeze fresh fruit and make sweet-and-sour mixes from scratch. The cruise line also has created a new menu of specialty cocktails that go far beyond frozen drinks. On certain cruises, guests can even attend cocktail demonstrations by master mixologists like

Raising the Bar

Tired of paying $14 for a cocktail? Here's what you need to make professional drinks without leaving home.

As the price of cocktails keeps climbing higher, it's increasingly tempting to stay at home and whip up your own. With the right tools and a good cocktail cookbook, it's actually pretty easy. To get you started, here's a list of everything you need to outfit your home bar.

Shaken, Not Stirred

Every bartender shakes drinks to his or her own beat. But there are only two kinds of cocktail shakers. One is called a Boston Shaker, which is made of two parts, a regular pint glass and what looks like a metal pint glass. The two parts are held together with pressure. The metal cup has a slightly larger diameter than the pint glass. Most professional bartenders use the Boston Shaker. If you use one, you'll need to buy a strainer to keep from pouring ice or fruit into your glass. (To get really professional, buy both the julep strainer, which looks like an oversized spoon with holes, and the Hawthorn strainer, which has a wire coil on its bottom to catch ice.)

The other shaker is the Cobbler Shaker, made from glass or metal, with a built-in strainer and a cap. The Cobbler Shaker is easy to buy (most housewares stores as well as places like Pottery Barn and Crate & Barrel stock them) and easy to use. The shaker is especially great for beginners because it doesn't come apart in the middle of shaking. But with a little practice, it's not hard to master the Boston Shaker.

Muddling Through

Drinkers love ordering mojitos and capirinhas, but bartenders hate making these cocktails. Why? These drinks take more time to prepare because some of the ingredients need to be "muddled." For instance, to make a mojito, you need to bruise the mint with a muddler, a long, wooden, bat-shaped device. Many of the best bartenders have recently switched over to the oversized Pug! Muddler ($30). The tool is hand turned from a selection of beautiful exotic woods. Besides its size, it also features a slanted top, like joystick, which allows you to exert a lot of downward pressure.

Ice Age

Even some of the fanciest bars ruin their drinks with inferior ice chips. The best bars go to great lengths to use super-cold, oversized ice cubes that won't melt in seconds and water down a drink. At home, you can achieve this by using old-fashioned ice trays that make big ice cubes.

The Glass Family

For every kind of cocktail, there's an appropriate glass. But if you want to keep it simple, make sure to have highball or chimney glasses for serving tall drinks, like Tom Collinses. You'll also need some lowball glasses for sipping scotch on the rocks or for an old-fashioned. And no bar is complete without a couple of good martini glasses.

The Right Book

Unless you're a pro or like to impress your friends, there's no need to memorize every cocktail recipe. In fact, the best cocktail cook

(continued)

books not only have recipes but offer tips, history, and facts that you can use to impress your guests. No bar should be without Dale DeGroff's award winning *The Craft of the Cocktail*. The book has tons of excellent drink recipes and offers a primer on cocktail history and preparation. Don't forget that many professional bartenders have been trained by DeGroff.

Julie Reiner, of New York's Flatiron Lounge, and Ryan Magarian, of Seattle's Liquid Kitchen.

Even though cocktails never totally disappeared, over the last five years, they've come back with a vengeance. And well-mixed pre-Prohibition cocktails aren't just being served on the East and West coasts anymore. Slowly, cocktails are making headway in the Midwest. Even the casual dining chain Applebee's offers a selection of specialty drinks and martinis. But "it's just going to take a while to catch on in those places," says Kim Haasarud, founder of drink consultancy Liquid Architecture and author of *101 Martinis*. A number of her clients have locations across the country. Sometimes when she comes up with a recipe that calls for fresh ingredients, her instructions "get lost in translation," and the bartenders make the drink using shortcuts.

But another encouraging sign that the trend will continue is that many young drinkers who have partied in clubs and bars that require bottle service are outgrowing simple mixed drinks. "At The Double Seven, we put the emphasis back on the 'crafted' cocktail," says David Rabin, president of the New York Nightlife Association and co-owner of The Double Seven. "We felt that as our customers 'grew up,' they'd want to experience these wonderfully made post-Prohibition era drinks with hand-cut ice blocks and freshly pressed juice." And instead of serving standard bar snacks, The Double Seven pairs its drinks with high-end chocolates. With so many delicious and innovative combinations, the cocktail is unlikely to disappear again.

CHAPTER FIVE

Courtesy of Maker's Mark

Welcome to the
Softer Side of Spirits

. . . .

IN CASE YOU haven't noticed, things have gotten a lot sweeter lately. On restaurant wine lists, very dry and oaky chardonnay and Chablis have been replaced by sweeter and fruitier wines, like sauvignon blanc and Rieslings. Bars are mixing up sweet pre-Prohibition cocktails made with fresh fruit juice and simple syrup. Health clubs and organic grocery stores are pushing so-called "healthy" smoothies made with sherbet and fruit. Even getting coffee has become a cavity-inducing experience. Care for a "cinnamon dolce" latte from Starbucks? It's a blend of espresso coffee, butter, brown sugar, and steamed whole milk topped with whipped cream and sprinkles. (A grande packs a whopping 440 calories and 22 grams of fat.)

Americans have always had a sweet tooth but they have become increasing greedy in their efforts to satisfy it. In fact, according to the U.S. Department of Agriculture, in 2005 per capita consumption of sugar and other sweeteners was 26 percent higher than in 1966. Reportedly, Americans now have the dubious distinction of consuming more sweeteners per capita than any other nation.

Drinkers have combined alcohol and sweeteners, like honey, for centuries. Plenty of sweet liqueurs and cordials have always been available to choose from, too, including Baileys, Chambord, and Kahlua. "Americans are known to talk dry and drink sweet," says Dean Phillips, president and CEO of Phillips Distilling Company. One reason for the recent success of the spirits industry has been a concerted effort by manufacturers to make their products more drinkable, which usually means sweeter and smoother.

The move now seems prescient, but the industry took a while to make this change. What helped kick-start the trend was the success of flavored vodkas in the late 1980s and the rebirth and the popularity of cocktails in the 1990s. Consumers are also now willing to pay more for complex-tasting spirits, which means distillers have the resources to pay for extra distillations, longer periods of aging, and better flavorings. These easy-drinking spirits especially appeal to consumers in their 20s and 30s who grew up buying sweet juices, sugary sodas, and sports drinks that taste like punch. It's no wonder that sweet spirits are increasingly popular.

Even the cordials and liqueurs category has seen a resurgence in sales during the last few years. Spurring this growth is the recent introduction of a number of interesting and pricey liqueurs, like Pama, a pomegranate liqueur ($25). According to the Distilled Spirits Council of the United States (DISCUS), only 1,000 nine-liter cases of super-premium cordials were sold in 2002. In 2005, that number was projected to increase by an amazing 2,200 percent for a total of 23,000 cases. (Over the same period, the overall cordial category increased by 7 percent.) And in 2005, cordials and liqueurs made up 12.5 percent of the overall America spirits market, just behind the vodka and rum categories.

These days, mixologists are using an ever-broader palate of flavors for their new drink creations, often turning to this new generation of liqueurs because they are so versatile. They can be sipped over ice, of course, but they are really perfect for adding flair to cocktails.

The category has become so popular that a number of whisky companies have produced liqueurs. In 1993, Godiva helped start the trend with the introduction of a line of fancy chocolate liqueurs it created with spirits giant Diageo. Just a few years ago, Suntory International, makers of Yamazaki whisky and Midori melon liqueur, came out with Zen Green Tea Liqueur. In 2005, Jim Beam partnered with Starbucks to produce a cream-coffee-flavored liqueur. In 2006, Wild Turkey launched a liqueur called American Honey ($19.99), which is very sweet but has notes of the company's famous bourbon. At 71 proof, American Honey is no lightweight. (The company actually introduced its first liqueur in 1976, and it has since gone through a number of adjustments and facelifts. According to Eddie Russell, director of barrel maturation and warehousing for Wild Turkey and son of the company's master distiller and legend Jimmy Russell, the product offered a way to compete with wine coolers.)

Even Macallan, perhaps the most revered Scottish single malt distiller, has come out with a liqueur. In 2005, the Macallan Amber, which has a maple-and-pecan flavor with a base of whisky, was tested in three American markets, including Boston and San Francisco. Wider distribution is planned for 2007. It's quite a change for the company, whose signature for many years was full-bodied whiskies. But it's not just whisky companies who are getting into the liqueurs market. Patrón, the super-premium tequila company, released XO Café, a coffee-flavored liqueur, in 1992; it now sells for about $23.

Whisky companies aren't just making liqueurs. They are also making their whisky smoother and sweeter. These changes are an attempt to appeal to a wider audience, including women and younger vodka drinkers. Another reason for changing recipes is that people now drink differently than they did just 20 years ago. As a result of tougher drunk-driving laws, people are drinking less and aren't just looking for the fastest way to get intoxicated. Between 1975 and 2005, according to DISCUS, adult per capita consumption of spirits decreased by over 35 percent. Now when people drink, they want a spirit that they can savor, especially if they only have one or two drinks. To take advantage of this trend, whisky companies are promoting their products as having more flavor and complexity.

Surely, whisky makers in Kentucky and Scotland have taken note of the recent success of Irish whiskey. According to DISCUS, from 1994 to 2005, nine-liter case sales of Irish whiskey in the United States have increased by a whopping 129 percent. Decades after almost completely disappearing from bars and liquor store shelves, the spirit staged a comeback in the mid-1990s with a sudden boom in Irish whiskey imports. These brands were a big hit with consumers because Irish whiskey is usually extremely smooth and has a sweet or honeyed taste, making it much easier to drink then fuller or smokier whiskies. And some of the Irish spirits, like the 12-year-old pot still Red Breast, are full of fruity cognac notes that are very appealing to non-whisky drinkers. This flavor profile comes from Irish distillers' triple distilling their whiskey, while Scottish distillers usually distill only twice. Also, traditionally when the Irish toast their malted barley, they make sure it doesn't come in contact with the smoke from the peat fire heating the kilns.

But change was afoot in Kentucky long before the rebirth of Irish whiskey. In 1943, Bill Samuels, Sr. burned his family's 170-year-old recipe for bourbon because he said he wanted a spirit that actually tasted good. He left his family distillery, T. W. Samuels, to form what would later become Maker's Mark. According to his son, Bill Samuels, Jr., the current president of Maker's Mark, he wanted a bourbon without sour notes that would hit you on the tip of your tongue where you taste sweetness. Historically, bourbons weren't

When Is a Whisky Not a Whiskey?

During the 1950s, blended whisky was king and made up over 50 percent of total spirit industry sales. But now there are all kinds of whisky: blended, single malt, Irish, and Canadian—not to mention American whiskey: bourbon and rye. So what's the difference among all of these whiskies? Here's a cheat sheet to help you keep your whiskies straight (or on the rocks).

Single Malt Whisky

Over the last 30 years, single malt whiskies have created a lot of buzz and taken over the top shelf of many bars. It's hard to find a bar that doesn't stock Glenlivet, Glenfiddich, or Macallan. A single malt is a blend of whisky from a single Scottish distillery. The whisky is made from Scottish malted barley and water. By law, to be called whisky, the spirit must be aged for at least three years in Scotland. If a bottle has an age of, for example, 12 years or 18 years, the whisky inside is at least that old. In Scotland, the word *whisky* is generally spelled without an *e*.

Blended Whisky

When most people order a blended whisky, they want a spirit like Chivas Regal, Dewar's, or Johnnie Walker. A blend contains a number of single malts from different distilleries. It's then blended with an aged grain whisky. Generally a blend contains between 15% and 60% single malt whisky, and the rest is grain whisky. Even though single malts have gotten more attention recently, blends still make up most of the total Scotch whisky sales.

(continued)

Irish Whiskey

Irish whiskey has seen a huge renaissance during the last ten years. Even though it was quite popular in the United States before Prohibition, for a number of decades, it practically disappeared from liquor stores and bars. Generally, the difference between Irish and Scottish whiskies is that Irish whiskey is distilled three times instead of twice. The extra distillation gives the spirit a slightly smoother taste. Also, Irish distillers generally don't smoke their malted barley with peat smoke as some of the Scottish distillers do. As a result, the Irish spirit has more of a honeyed taste. When talking about whiskey from Ireland, you spell the word with an *e*.

Canadian Whisky

Canada has been producing whisky for over 200 years. The country's Scottish immigrants brought with them a distilling expertise and an appetite for whisky. Canadian whisky blends, which were popular during Prohibition and then had a resurgence in the 1980s, are generally made from corn, barley, and rye. Because the whisky has a signature spicy flavor caused by the rye component, it's sometimes simply called rye whisky.

American Whiskey

In America, whiskey is usually called bourbon or rye. Bourbon has to be made from at least 51 percent corn. Usually the rest is rye or wheat. (Jack Daniel's, however, is not technically bourbon but Tennessee whiskey because it's charcoal filtered.) The rules for making rye are a little looser, and the spirit can be made from 100 percent rye. When talking about American whiskey, you usually spell the word with an *e*.

known for their subtlety or flavor but for their potency. "My ancestors wanted to blow your ears off," says Bill Samuels, Jr. According to Dave Pickerell, the current master distiller at Maker's Mark, "When [Samuels] started making Maker's Mark, no one cared what bourbon tasted like." After eight years of experimenting, Samuels was finally able to come up with a recipe that produced what Pickerell says is a bourbon that's "pleasant, sweet, and nonoffensive. And that's not an acquired taste." The whiskey appeals to a wide range of drinkers. The sweetness also means the spirit is easily mixed in cocktails.

By 1958, Maker's Mark's distinctive bottles, hand dipped in red wax, were on store shelves selling for $7. So how did Samuels create this sweeter spirit? For one, the bourbon is made from corn and wheat, which gives the spirit a bit of sweetness. Most other bourbons are made from corn and rye, which produces a spirit with a bitter kick. According to legend, Samuels didn't develop this recipe in a distillery but in his kitchen. He experimented by baking bread with different grain combinations. Maker's Mark was also much smoother than it competitors because the company decided to age the spirit in barrels longer—generally between 5 years and 11 months to 7 years and 1 month. (While technically a spirit can be called bourbon if it's aged just two years, most are usually aged for four years.) As a result of aging and the way the spirit is distilled, Maker's Mark was also bottled at a lower proof (90) than many other bourbons, which top a hefty 100 proof.

According to Pickerell, at first the rest of the industry treated Samuels like a Kentucky Don Quixote. His friends were willing to indulge him and help him create a better-tasting bourbon because "they never thought it would amount to anything." Part of the industry's hesitation to change was based on fiscal considerations. It costs a lot more to age bourbon and to distill it at a lower proof. It's more cost-effective to produce higher-proof bourbon and then cut it with water, resulting in more bottles to sell. But Samuels's developments

proved quite wise. Over the decades that followed, partially to compete with vodka, the rest of the industry slowly began introducing
products that were of a lower proof and aged for longer period of
time. (Maker's Mark, of course, takes credit for creating this new
flavor profile, but surely the other companies would disagree.)

In the late 1980s, when expensive Scottish single malts began
taking up more room on liquor store shelves, the bourbon industry
began to focus on producing higher-quality spirits that would rival
Scotch in complexity, flavor, and price. "We started to see American
consumers starting to spend a lot of money on good whiskey," says
Chris Morris, master distiller at Woodford Reserve. The introduction of Jim Beam's Small Batch Bourbon Collection helped create
this trend. In 1988, Booker Noe, the master distiller at Jim Beam
and an industry legend, created Booker's bourbon, the first batch
of which was given out to distributors "to see if there was interest
in the product," says Booker's son Fred Noe, the Jim Beam brand
ambassador and an associate distiller. The bourbon, which is still
available, is a full-flavored whiskey that's been aged between six and
eight years. (It's quite strong, between 121 and 127 proof, because
Booker thought people should water it down themselves to taste.)
Booker's went on sale in 1989, and its success was important because
it showed the industry that consumers were willing to pay more, up
to $50, for a better bottle of bourbon. "The future is high-end," says
Fred Noe. This has ushered in an era of high-priced, small-batch
bourbon that bears scant resemblance to the spirit's origins. In 1992,
Jim Beam added an additional three brands to the Small Batch Bourbon Collection. Not to be outdone, in 1991, Wild Turkey released
Rare Breed, a barrel proof premium bourbon, which sells for $32.99.
To take advantage of this new market, in 1996, Brown-Forman created a new bourbon brand called Woodford Reserve. The company
"didn't want it to be low priced," says Morris. "We wanted it to be
ultra-premium." At the time, Woodford Reserve's $29.99 price tag

made it expensive. In 2006, Morris created a special, limited edition bourbon (there are only a total of 750 cases) uniquely made from four grains, which sells for $79.99. It's the first release from a new line of higher-end bourbons called the Master's Collection.

Maker's Mark isn't the only whiskey to use wheat to sweeten its product. In the fall of 2005, Heaven Hill, known for its Evan Williams bourbon and Christian Brothers brandy, introduced Bernheim Original Kentucky Straight Wheat Whiskey ($39.99). According to the company, it's the only spirit to be made mostly from wheat. (The recipe also calls for some corn and malted barley.) The recipe is so distinctive that Heaven Hill is calling it a whole new whiskey category. The winter wheat the company uses makes the spirit sweeter than if it had been made with rye. The hope is that the spirit appeals more to nonwhisky drinkers. Bernheim launched in 12 markets across the country, including New York, Florida, and Illinois, and the company now says the whiskey is available across the country.

According to spirits experts and industry veterans, it seems that bourbon companies have been very successful in broadening the spirit's appeal. "Bourbon was considered your dad's drink or your granddad's drink," says Fred Noe. Now bourbon drinkers are often younger and, even more encouraging, female. "I think someplace down the road, girls won't get funny looks when they order bourbon," he says. And this push has indeed helped increase sales of bourbon and Tennessee whiskey. From 2000 to 2005, according to DISCUS, sales of these whiskies in the United States were up almost 7 percent. That is quite impressive considering that since the early 1970s, bourbon and Tennessee whiskey sales were steadily declining.

Even though the Scotch whisky distillers have been on a roll, they're also looking to attract new drinkers and diversify their offerings. Distillers can relatively easily change the flavor and smoothness of their whisky without changing their recipes. They can do it by changing the cask in which the spirit is aged. The barrel actually

Jimmy Russell: American Bourbon Royalty

For over half a century, Jimmy Russell has been making Wild Turkey Bourbon.

It's hard to separate the history of Jimmy Russell's family from the history of Wild Turkey Bourbon. Four generations of Russell men have worked in the Lawrenceburg, Kentucky, distillery, crafting one of the most famous American spirits. You could say that bourbon is in Jimmy Russell's blood.

This living bourbon legend and master distiller was born and raised just a few miles from the distillery. Russell always wanted to work in the bourbon business and hoped to get a job at one of the four local distilleries. In 1954, when he turned 20, he went to work at Wild Turkey, and he never left. It was his "first real job," he says, and keeping with tradition, he started at the bottom doing quality control. He inspected and sometimes unloaded the grains delivered to the distillery. Slowly he moved up through the ranks, eventually training under the brand's master distiller, Bill Hughes.

Russell replaced Hughes in the late 1960s, becoming only the third person ever to hold the title of master distiller at the company. At the time, the brand was really just one product: Wild Turkey 101. Over the last half century, Russell created a full line of different bourbons that now includes five more varieties of Wild Turkey, including a lower-octane 80-proof bourbon, a bourbon-based liqueur with honey, and a single-barrel bourbon.

But perhaps the most distinctive bourbon Jimmy created is the one that bears his name. In 2000, Wild Turkey introduced the ten-year-old Russell's Reserve. The bourbon is a testament to the Russell family's legacy and their dedication to the spirit. What also makes the bottling special is that Jimmy worked on the bourbon with his son Eddie, who has worked at Wild Turkey for 26 years and is the company's barrel maturation and warehousing manager.

Just a few years later, in honor of Jimmy's 50th year on the job, Wild Turkey released 5,500 bottles of a small-batch, 15-year-old bourbon. Fittingly, the bottling was called Tribute.

contributes a lot to the finished spirit, including its color. In fact, the whisky is clear when it comes out of the still and only picks up its deep honey or mahogany color from the wood. But the barrel is not just about aesthetics. The wood of the barrel and what the barrel previously held also affect the flavor of the whiskey. The Edrington Group, which owns Macallan and Highland Park, estimates that as much as 80 percent of a whisky's flavor comes from the barrel.

Historically, the distilleries have bought used barrels, which are cheaper. For decades they were plentiful because many items, from wine to dry goods, were shipped in barrels. Then a law was passed in the 1960s dictating that bourbon distillers could only use new charred barrels, which ensured that the market was flooded with relatively cheap American oak barrels. (Sherry casks are about ten times more expensive than bourbon casks.) Until the late 1980s, distillers almost exclusively used former bourbon and sherry barrels.

That all changed when Scottish distilleries started selling their single malt whisky to consumers. In hopes of distinguishing their product from all the other whiskies on the market, some distilleries started experimenting with aging their whisky in different types of casks. Distillers realized that barrels that once held wine, Madera and port, gave their whiskies more flavor. The whisky can pick up fruity or spicy notes from the wine-soaked wood, and it can become a bit smoother.

Finishing whiskies in wine casks has become a standard in the industry, often for special limited editions that are especially popular with collectors. Whisky aged in former wine casks is generally easier to drink and popular with people who don't normally order Scotch. Usually the whisky is moved from bourbon barrels into wine casks for the last few years of maturation. Some distilleries have also experimented with finishing whisky in casks that have held other spirits. In 2006, Glenfiddich introduced a 21-year-old Gran Reserva ($120) that was aged in a cask that had held rum.

This style of whisky has become the signature of Glenmorangie: no other distillery has experimented as much with aging whisky in different casks. For three years during the early 1990s, Glenmorangie monitored over 10,000 different casks to see how various types of wood affect the taste of whisky. Traditionally, distillers would only finish poor whisky in a different cask in hopes of improving its quality. But according to Glenmorangie's master distiller Bill Lumsden, the brand began experimenting with finishing its best whisky. "It's an interesting and valid way to give consumers something different," says Lumsden. Finishing is "one of the most powerful tools to give a range of flavors." The brand has used a number of different types of casks, including ones that have held Malaga, port, Madeira, and Burgundy. And like former bourbon barrels, these wine casks allow the character of the whisky to come through in the final product. In 2006, Glenmorangie introduced a whisky that was finished for two years in a wine cask that came from Bordeaux's Margaux commune. Just 3,551 bottles of this special Glenmorangie were made, and only 720 were allocated for sale in the United States. The company expected the whisky to sell for between $399 and $499 per bottle. So far, the company has had a lot of success with these limited edition bottlings; each has sold out completely.

Some Scotch whisky companies have gone in a different direction to attract a broader range of consumers. For 180 years, Macallan only used sherry casks to age its whisky. The wood became the company's signature, because the rest of the industry for the most part used old bourbon barrels. In fact, Macallan is the only Scottish distillery that has all its barrels specially constructed. Every year, the company buys oak trees grown in Spain that are at least 80 years old. According to brand ambassador Caspar MacRae, as little as 15 percent of the wood from these trees meets the whisky company's high standards and is turned into barrel staves. (The rest of the wood goes to the local community.) The wood is sun-dried, and then Macallan pays a Spanish sherry maker to fill the casks with oloroso sherry. After several years of use, the barrels are sent to Macallan's distillery in Speyside to be filled with whisky. Even though Macallan doesn't get to keep the sherry, each barrel has soaked up as much as 11 liters of it. The company takes wood selection so seriously that the distillery recently opened an educational exhibit on the subject. "Macallan made its name from sherry casks," says MacRae.

One summer night back in 2004, in front of a packed crowd in the ballroom of a hip midtown Manhattan hotel, Macallan's distiller Bob Dalgarno shocked the spirits world by announcing a revolutionary new line called Fine Oak. This whisky broke with company tradition, using both sherry and American oak bourbon barrels. The company had actually been making this style of whisky for years but selling it only to blenders. It's no surprise that Macallan released the whisky to the public. The hallmark of the most popular Scottish whisky, Glenlivet and Glenfiddich, and many of the other distilleries in Speyside, is a lighter and fruitier style that derives from American oak-barrel aging. The company was banking on a smoother and lighter Macallan to appeal to a wider range of both whisky and non-whisky drinkers. "Fine Oak is part of making Macallan more approachable," says MacRae. "It's more of an aperitif style." The Fine Oak's pricing was also appealing to both sets of potential consumers. The younger Fine Oak whiskies are less expensive than the comparable traditional Sherry Oak whiskies. But for the collector, the 30-year-old Fine Oak sells for between $650 and $850.

Macallan's former master distiller David Robertson made an even more aggressive attempt to attract new whisky drinkers. Several years ago, he started a brand that's now called the Easy Drinking Whisky Company. (He mixed the first batches in his kitchen.) The idea behind the new brand was to strip away all the wonkish nomenclature and focus on making extremely consumer-friendly whisky. When it was introduced to the American market in the summer of 2005, Robertson was quoted in a company release as saying: "We've completely chucked the whisky rule book. So you can toss your tie and drink it where you like, when you like, and how you like." To help consumers figure out what the whisky actually tasted like, the three varieties were simply called: The Rich Spicy One, The Smokey Peaty One, and The Smooth Sweeter One. This is obviously a departure from the way Scotch is traditionally labeled by age and distillery name. Just as complicated French wine labels can be intimidating, so too can those of Scotch whisky bottles. It's no wonder that a number of distillers, like Australian wineries, have experimented with giving different whiskies actual names and eye-catching packaging.

But it's not just the labels of the Easy Drinking Whisky Company's bottles that are unique. What's inside is also innovative. The Smooth Sweeter One is a blend of two whiskies, one from the Scottish Bunnahabhain Distillery and the other from the Irish Cooley Distillery. This mixture is then aged in a bourbon cask. The price of the brand's whiskies is also refreshingly low: each bottle sells for just $29.99. "We're not about paying $50 or $60 a bottle," says the brand manager, Stephen Cruty.

Even though Robertson has since left the company, sales of Easy Drinking Whisky continue to grow steadily. According to Cruty, the brand is particularly popular in places where there is a strong microbrew and microdistilling culture, like Austin, Texas; California; and Colorado. But the growth of the whisky is still very much a grassroots movement, and the company doesn't have any illusions of becoming huge. "It's a niche brand," admits Cruty. But one reason why the whisky is successfully making whisky converts out of vodka drinkers is because it mixes so well in cocktails. Drinkers can even find recipes on the company's website, including one for the Smokey Cokey (a mixture of The Smokey Peaty One and cola) and for the Sweet Ginger Fizz (a mixture of the Smooth Sweeter One and ginger beer).

A key to whiskey marketing now is creating cocktails based on the spirit. A number of companies have gone even further. They are making products that are not only sweeter and smoother but also better complement soda or other mixers. It's a revolutionary idea, because for years, Scotch whisky and bourbon experts and enthusiasts have insisted that these spirits only be drunk straight or, if you insist, mixed with a little bottled water. In May 2005, the Minneapolis-based Phillips Distilling Company, which claims to have produced America's first peppermint-flavored schnapps brand in the 1930s, introduced a new line of flavored whiskies. According to CEO Dean Phillips, a member of the fifth generation of his family to work in the spirits business, he was looking for a way to shake up the category and "convert younger vodka drinkers to whiskey." The new line of whiskey, called Phillips Union, is particularly smooth because it's made from a unique blend of Kentucky bourbon and Canadian whisky. (It's the first whiskey on the market to blend these spirits.) In addition to the regular Phillips Union whiskey, there are also two flavored versions: a cherry and a vanilla. The company chose these two flavors because they mix well with cola and in cocktails. "Not that many flavors mix well with whiskey," Phillips admits.

So far, the line has sold well and is available in 30 states, including California and Illinois. The company produced 20,000 cases during the brand's first year, and they sold out. Slowly Phillips plans to increase production by about 10 percent to 15 percent per year, building up to about 30,000 cases. These sales are particularly impressive because the company isn't targeting whisky drinkers. This is a "whiskey that traditionalists won't buy or appreciate," Phillips says. But young people will. According to Phillips, consumers won't spend a lot of money on a flavored spirit, whether it is whisky or vodka. "When consumers pay a premium, they are buying purity," he says. The best-selling flavored spirits are midpriced or less and are popular with younger people who often have less to spend on a bottle and aren't looking for a sipping whisky. Phillips Union has a suggested retail price of $25, which is perhaps a little more than value vodka but about $5 cheaper than the premium vodkas like Grey Goose.

Phillips wants consumers to view this line almost like a whole new product category and not just a type of whisky. Even the packaging of the line is quite different than the way whisky has traditionally been bottled and labeled. For one, the company uses a distinctive clear, flasklike bottle that features lettering in a funky font and a hip logo. The packaging looks more like that of a fancy bottled water than a whiskey. Phillips Union has its own website, which is obviously geared to a young audience. The site tries to create the feel of being in a club or bar. When you click on an image, you hear crowd noise, people softly talking, and drinks being poured. And like any good bar, the website offers its own soundtrack of upbeat funky acoustic music. The site provocatively asks "So are you and vodka taking a break?" and "Does vodka know you go both ways?"

Even where companies don't change the recipe of their spirits to make them more mixable, they suggest that their product be consumed in new ways. Fred Noe says, "A lot of people would say it's a sin to mix a high-end bourbon with coke." But it's no sin to him. To

The New Bourbon Royalty

In the bourbon world, *new* is a relative term. The basic recipe hasn't changed since the late 1700s, when early American settlers began producing the spirit using their excess corn. But change is afoot in bourbon country thanks to a new generation of whiskey makers, like Eddie Russell of Wild Turkey, Fred Noe of Jim Beam, Craig Beam of Heaven Hill, Chris Morris of Woodford Reserve, and Dave Pickerell of Maker's Mark, who are taking over the distilleries.

New is also relative, given that these men have already worked in the industry for many years. Russell has been working at Wild Turkey for 26 years. Noe has been at Jim Beam for almost as long. (Not to mention all those years that the two hung around the distilleries as kids with their fathers.) This changing of the guard is a rare occurrence because bourbon careers are often longer than many real monarchies. The Queen of England has only a year on Wild Turkey master distiller and Eddie Russell's father, Jimmy Russell.

And like royalty, the bourbon business has traditionally been a family business. Many of the men running the different houses have followed in the footsteps of their fathers and their father's fathers, sometimes going all the way back to when Kentucky wasn't part of the United States and bourbon was an illicit spirit made by immigrants fleeing the government's punitive whiskey taxes. These different bourbon families joined together to form an ad hoc family tree, with each branch a different brand. And many of the people making bourbon literally are relatives. The Beams of Heaven Hill and the Noes of Jim Beam are descended from the same family. According to Craig Beam, at one point, it was said that there was at least one Beam at every bourbon distillery.

(continued)

To this day, the business is "more like a brotherhood," says Noe. The master distillers are on friendly terms and usually get together for lunch a few times a year to talk shop. And because the design of all the distilleries is pretty similar, if one distiller needs a part, like a ball bearing, it's not uncommon for another distiller to lend him one. "We let the marketing or salespeople fight it out in the field," says Craig Beam.

However, in recent years, some new names have been added to the "family tree." As the spirits world has become increasingly corporate, many of the family businesses have been sold to big companies. Master distillers who grew up outside this tight-knit, insular world have been chosen to lead some of these bourbon houses. But only slowly have these people been accepted into the bourbon fraternity. "Maybe we've just changed the definition of family a little bit," says Pickerell, who started out as a chemical engineer and hopes that some new bourbon dynasties may soon form. "Maybe we could start another one up."

To help you get acquainted with the new generation, you've got to know about four of its leading members.

Craig Beam of Heaven Hill

With a last name of Beam, the odds were pretty good that Craig Beam would join the family business making bourbon at Heaven Hill. He's the seventh generation of his family to make whiskey. But before signing on, Beam seriously considered becoming a veterinarian. Fortunately for whiskey drinkers, the number of years of school required to become a vet scared him into rethinking his career path. Beam was also comfortable in the Heaven Hill distillery, because as a child he would visit his father and grandfather at work. Beam began working for Heaven Hill in the summers during college. One of his first projects was evicting a flock of pigeons that had been squatting in an old warehouse owned by the company. Needless to say, there was a lot to clean up after the birds were relocated. Another summer he worked in the bottling house. In 1983, Beam officially joined the company. His grandfather and his father carefully taught him the business, including how to make the family's traditional yeast strain. Up until the end of his grandfather's life, Craig brought him samples of the "jug yeast" and the "white dog" (unaged alcohol that has come straight from the still) to taste.

Now Craig's father, Parker Beam, is semiretired, and they share the title of master distiller. Inheriting Heaven Hill is a huge job. Unlike most of its competitors, the company is still family owned. That means Beam not only has to oversee production of the company's vast portfolio of whiskies but is also involved in every aspect of the business, including negotiating trucking contracts, warehousing, and buying grains. With the increased interest in spirits, Heaven Hill also has had "a lot of growing pains," says Beam. The distillery where the bourbon, rye, and wheat whiskey is produced runs 12 hours a day, 6 days a week. Demand is so strong that by early 2008, the size of the distillery will almost double. Beam has also begun bringing around his two teenage daughters, hoping that one of them may want to join him in the family business. "Maybe one of them will be the first female master distiller," Beam says. "You never know."

Eddie Russell of Wild Turkey

Eddie Russell never thought that he would join the family bourbon business at Wild Turkey. But after graduating from the University of Kentucky, he decided to join his father at the distillery, becoming the fourth generation of his family to work in the bourbon

(continued)

business. He started out doing odd jobs like mowing grass and dumping bottles.

Almost three decades later, Eddie is now the director of barrel maturation and warehousing. He's taking a bigger role in making the bourbon because his father, Master Distiller Jimmy Russell, is often on the road to promote the brand around the world. In 2000, Eddie and Jimmy worked together on the excellent ten-year-old Russell's Reserve.

Fred Noe of Jim Beam

After finishing college in 1983, Fred Noe was hired by the Jim Beam distillery as the company's night-shift bottling supervisor. He wasn't just any new hire. He is the seventh generation of his family to work in the bourbon business. When Jacob Beam began selling his whisky in 1795, Kentucky had only been a state for three years. After Prohibition was repealed, Fred Noe's great-grandfather, Jim Beam, constructed the company's distillery.

Fred literally grew up surrounded by bourbon history. As a child, he lived in Jim Beam's former home, and he would often accompany his father, bourbon legend Booker Noe, to the distillery on the weekends. While Booker worked, Fred would play on the company's trucks or watch the trains go by. "Back when I was a kid, that was big time," he remembers. "The distillery was always a comfort zone." Fred says his father didn't force him into the family business but let him decide for himself. And Booker insisted that Fred go to college and get a degree.

Even when Fred signed on, Booker still wanted to be sure he was serious. His first job overseeing the distillery's bottling line overnight wasn't easy. "I think it was a test," says Fred. If it was, Fred must have passed. In two decades at Jim Beam, Fred has steadily moved up the ladder and is currently an associate distiller and brand ambassador. He hopes that his own son may follow in his footsteps. "There may be a new generation yet," he says.

Dave Pickerell of Maker's Mark

By the ripe old age of five, Dave Pickerell knew he wanted to be a chemical engineer. The desire was so strong that in high school, he took every math and science course the school offered, even attending summer school to cram them all in. He applied to and was accepted at West Point. Although the school didn't have a chemical engineering department, it offered him something even more important: a full scholarship. Pickerell admits that without it, he might never have been able go to college.

He soon realized that he was particularly good at thermodynamics. "Somehow I am wired to get this," he says. After finishing up his degree, he spent about six years working for a thermodynamic company consulting on distilleries, including Maker's Mark. In 1994, the company called him to offer him a job. "I couldn't say yes fast enough," he remembers. Bourbon "gets in your blood, and you can't get it out."

But in the early 1990s, bourbon was still very much a family business. "I was the first of the new guys." And because of that distinction, "I was certainly an outsider," he says. "People saw me as a hired gun, and I had to earn my spot." Today no one questions Pickerell's skills or dedication. In fact, he's now one of the more senior distillers. Pickerell has become an expert's expert on the production of bourbon and serves as a board member of the Kentucky Distillers' Association. He heads up the Association's technical committee as well.

(continued)

He's not related to the Samuels family that started Maker's Mark, but he is planning to continue their legacy. Even if one of his children doesn't join the business, Pickerell has been mentoring an employee for 15 years to take over when he retires. And for the last three years, he's been mentoring another employee who could take over the distillery even further down the road. "I hope we can keep this alive," he says.

Noe, it's just "the best bourbon and coke." In his mind, too many brands have too many rules about how people should drink whiskey. "We don't like rules in Kentucky," he says. "Drink it anyway you want. Mix it any way you want." In fact, the Jim Beam website has over 50 recipes for cocktails, like the Jim Beam "weekend punch," which calls for four different juices and ginger ale, and the Jim Beam "black coffee & creamtini," which is a mixture of bourbon, Starbucks coffee liqueur, and Irish cream.

Noe isn't alone. There's even some dissension in Scotland, which has been known for its strict rules about how whisky should—and certainly how it should not—be drunk. Douglas McLean Murray, master of whisky at Johnnie Walker, echoes Noe's sentiments and says you can drink his blends "any way you want." He hates being told you can't add water or ice to your whisky and calls it his pet peeve. "You'll never waste the whisky by adding water," he says. He even likes to make mixed drinks with Johnnie Walker Green Label ($45–$55). But for a real treat, he'll pour a little bit of chilled Gold Label ($75–$80) and chocolate sauce onto vanilla ice cream. (He uses this trick, he says, when he has to break some bad news to his wife.) But even Murray draws the line when it comes to certain special single malts. "Blue Label is the exception to the rule," he says. "I would never mix Blue with water." He usually cleanses his palate with a drink of water before drinking the rare and expensive ($200) whisky.

Still, clearly an increasing number of whiskey companies are making spirits that can be more easily mixed. And even those spirits that can't be mixed are being made more palatable and more complex to attract a wider range of drinkers. Soon, says Dave Pickerell, Maker's Mark master distiller, your drink may become spicy. "The American palate is migrating to be more sweet and will move on to savory," he says. "The next thing coming down the pipe is spices." People usually start with sweeter flavors but as their palates get more experienced and mature, they begin gravitating to more bitter and complex tasting spirits. (The same process usually happens with people who eat a lot of chocolate. They start out eating sweeter milk chocolate, and as their palates get more refined, they begin gravitating to increasingly darker and often more expensive chocolate.) This may explain the increasing popularity of rye whiskey and the super-peaty Scottish single malts from Islay, like Lagavulin and Laphroaig. They are an acquired taste and have a very select following. But like dark chocolate, they also offer a lot of flavor and a bold taste.

Already, Pickerell has seen bars in London making cocktails with simple syrup that has been flavored with herbs or spices, like rosemary and jasmine. Savory cocktails have been appearing on this side of the Pond as well. One of the first restaurants to start the trend was New York City's Tabla. When Danny Meyer opened Tabla in 1998, the restaurant's innovative cocktails got a lot of press. Playing off the restaurant's Indian-fusion cuisine, the drinks include exotic ingredients like lemongrass-infused fresh pineapple juice, red bell pepper vodka, green chilies, cucumber, cilantro, and tamarind.

New cookbooks contain recipes for making savory simple syrup. In Food Network host Dave Lieberman's 2006 book, *Dave's Dinners,*

The Return of Rye

The original American spirit is staging an epic comeback.

Just as France is known for its cognac and Scotland is famous for its whisky, America's signature spirit for decades was rye. The dark, flavorful alcohol was made by some the country's earliest residents, including George Washington, whose distillery produced thousands of gallons. Up until Prohibition, rye was widely available and made by quite a few different distilleries. On the rocks, and on screen, the spirit was a favorite of tough guys and working Joes. It was also popular with bartenders, who used it in many famous cocktails like the Manhattan, the old-fashioned, and the Sazerac.

However, after Prohibition ended, sales of rye began to decline. By the late 1990s, the spirit had almost completely disappeared from store shelves and was treated like a relic cherished only by a handful of diehard fans. Fortunately, starting around the millennium, rye was adopted by spirit connoisseurs and foodies as a cause célèbre. As a result, rye sales are up, and distilleries are steadily increasing production. Suddenly there's an ever-growing selection of rye produced by a number of different brands. Rye's comeback is nothing short of miraculous and proof of the current popularity of spirits.

But you can't have a dramatic comeback without a downfall. So why was rye overlooked for so many decades? There are many theories about rye's decline; the real cause is a combination of factors. Even though most of the rye today is made in Kentucky by the bourbon companies, traditionally the spirit was made in the mid-Atlantic states. According to Allen Katz, chairman of the board of Slow Food USA and director of mixology and spirits education for Southern Wine & Spirits of New York, after Prohibition ended, these states enacted some of the strictest laws regarding the production and sale of spirits. These laws made starting up difficult for rye distillers. Plus after being dormant for so many years, the different brands also had no stock of aged whiskey that could be bottled immediately and sold. It would take a few years before the first bottles would reach consumers. Meanwhile consumers began drinking other kinds of spirits that were readily available.

No sooner had the distilleries reopened than they had to shut down for World War II. The postwar period presented the same challenges that distillers had faced after Prohibition plus some new ones. The "GIs came back, and they had a taste for Scotch," says Larry Kass, spokesperson for Heaven Hill, one of the largest producers of rye in the United States. At the same time, the postwar boom industrialized much of the mid-Atlantic, cutting off distillers' local supply of rye and other grains.

As a result, the bourbon distilleries began producing a token amount of rye. "We spill more bourbon in a day," jokes Kass. Heaven Hill isn't alone. For example, Jim Beam sold just over 30,000 cases of rye in 2005, while it sold 3.9 million cases of bourbon that year. Even though rye is a tiny category, the Kentucky distillers continued to produce the spirit out of obligation. "We kept the category alive," says Kass. "We didn't think much of it." The two spirits are also very similar. Bourbon is made mostly from corn and often some rye. Rye is, of course, made mostly from rye, but can contain some corn. Producing rye is a bit harder than making bourbon, because the mash (the grains mixed up with water) is very sticky and runs through the still at a much slower pace. Until recently, only three main distilleries were producing rye, which was sold under a handful of labels. For decades, Heaven Hill made rye only two days a year, which was more than enough to satisfy demand. In fact, in

(continued)

many years, even this was too much. The company kept the extra whiskey in its storehouse where the rye sat undisturbed for years. Now it seems like a prescient move, because for the first time in decades, there's a real demand for aged rye.

A change in consumer taste also hurt rye sales. Smoother spirits, including blended whisky, bourbon, and even the white spirits, became much more popular after the war. And in the second half of the century, vodka stole an increasingly larger market share, acquiring more shelf space in liquor stores. The success of vodka came at the expense of the overall whiskey category but hurt rye in particular. Vodka was new and exciting for Americans. The clear, tasteless spirit can, of course, be mixed easily with virtually anything. It is also the polar opposite of rye, which is dark and full of bold flavors, making no apologies. And you can forget trying to hide the taste of rye in a sweet or fruity cocktail. Compared to vodka, rye seemed out-of-date and inextricably linked to a bygone era. And worst of all, it acquired the connotation of being a drink of the old.

By the late 1990s, rye was virtually unknown. "You'd say 'I'll have a rye Manhattan,' and they would pull out Canadian Club," says Katz. Many drinkers and bartenders began to confuse Canadian whisky, which does contain a lot of rye, with rye whiskey. Kass also puts some of the blame for the spirit's low profile on the distillers for not properly marketing the spirit. "We shot ourselves in the foot," he says.

It seemed that rye was destined to fade into the annals of history. But just as the spirit had been doomed by a confluence of international events, a number of factors helped to make the spirit popular again. It was a "perfect storm of factors drawing people to rye," says Kass. Even though rye was traditionally an American alcohol, some of the first people to begin talking and writing about it were members of the international press. The fact that the spirit wasn't widely available in foreign countries made it particularly alluring. These early articles got people in America to start thinking and talking about rye.

The spirit was also helped by American's burgeoning interest in bourbon and Scotch whisky. People who had once been satisfied with drinking simple vodka cocktails were soon buying so-called brown spirits. What really helped to attract customers was the pricey single malts and the small-batch boutique bourbons that Jim Beam and the other brands began producing. As drinkers began to get more familiar with these high-end whiskies, their level of connoisseurship began to rise. Suddenly, there was a cachet to drinking expensive, limited-edition whiskies from very small distilleries. And as people's palates developed, they began looking for spirits with ever more flavor and complexity. (This also accounts for the growing popularity of very smoky, peaty Scottish whisky.)

During the same period, the cocktail boom began to pick up steam, and bartenders and mixologists started promoting authentic pre-Prohibition drinks. A key element to making these drinks was getting the details right and using the correct spirits, not just substituting vodka or bourbon. Many of the earliest proponents of rye were bartenders who insisted on making their Manhattans with only that spirit. These cocktails introduced or reintroduced many drinkers to rye.

Then in the early 1990s, Fritz Maytag, owner of the legendary, pioneering San Francisco microbrew Anchor Steam Beer, began experimenting with making a boutique rye whiskey. At the time, it seemed like the vanity project of an eccentric. (To his credit, the same could have been said when Maytag took over the beer

(continued)

brewery in the 1960s.) In 1996, he released fewer than 1,500 bottles of Old Potrero Single Malt Whiskey, a special 100 percent rye malt, aged for about a year in toasted new barrels. Because the supply was so small, the whiskey was initially available only to local restaurants, but critics and drinkers soon began clamoring for the spirit. It was unlike any other rye on the market, because it was made using 18th-century distilling techniques. It was also packaged in an eye-catching, old-school squat bottle. Over the next ten years, Maytag started making Old Potrero Straight Rye Whiskey, which is aged for three years in new charred barrels, and Old Potrero Single Malt Hotaling's Whiskey, which has been aged for 11 years in once-used charred oak barrels. The introduction of these high-quality whiskies got the industry excited about the possibilities of making and selling rye whiskey. And Maytag's name lent a certain coolness and seriousness to the spirit category.

Rye was also a marketer's dream. It had a great back story, and it was old enough to be new to many drinkers. The fact that its supply was limited and not widely stocked only added to its allure. The spirit also was adopted by foodies and groups like Slow Food. Just like grass-fed beef, free-range chicken, and heirloom tomatoes, rye was a throwback worth saving from extinction. What had originally hurt sales of the spirit ultimately helped to bring it back. Suddenly drinkers and journalists were praising the spirit's flavor and writing about its long history. Rye seems particularly interesting compared to the mass-produced vodkas that have come to dominate the market. In late November 2006, the *New York Times* ran a "Spirits of the Times" column about rye, which included a report on the tasting of 15 brands. Many of the ryes the panel tasted cost around $100, a staggering sum given that just a few years before, it had been hard to find even a $15 bottle in most liquor stores. Just like with the rest of the industry, over the next few years, an increasing number of premium and super-premium ryes will likely be introduced.

Rye whiskies have also begun winning awards at spirits competitions. On a whim in 2006, Heaven Hill entered its $13 Rittenhouse Rye into the San Francisco World Spirits Competition. The bargain-priced rye shocked the industry by taking home top honors: North American Whiskey of the Year. It not only beat out other ryes but other double-gold-medal-winning whiskies in different spirit categories. It's no wonder that the rye was awarded the "Best Buy of the Year" award at the 2006 *Malt Advocate* New York WhiskyFest. The success of the brand prompted Heaven Hill to release a $150 100-proof, 21-year-old, single-barrel Rittenhouse Rye. Fortunately decades ago, the company had stored the rye on a lower floor of a warehouse, which offered an ideal aging environment. This premium spirit has become so popular, the company has had trouble keeping up with demand.

Now distillers are facing a new problem: too much demand. According to DISCUS, their members were projected to sell 50,000 cases of rye in 2006, an increase of 38 percent since 2000. (And that statistic doesn't include the figures from the Heaven Hill distillery, which is family owned and not part of DISCUS.) Some brands are seeing even larger increases. Shipments of nine-liter cases of Jim Beam's Old Overholt were up 43 percent from 2001 to 2006.

At this point, there isn't enough supply to keep up with current sales levels, and the brands are trying to catch up. Many companies have doubled their output. But because rye has to be aged, the supply will take a few years to make it onto store shelves. Not only are consumers scrambling to buy the spirit, but the wholesale market has also heated up. Distillers now routinely

(continued)

field offers from a number of companies who are trying to buy casks to rebottle under their own brand names. Joining Anchor Steam Distilling, a number of smaller companies are now making new rye brands as well.

The spirit is so popular that liquor stores are again devoting shelf space to rye. One of the best selections can be found in LeNell's, a liquor store in the Red Hook neighborhood of Brooklyn, New York. The store stocks 21 different bottles of rye that range in price from $13.50 to $150. The selection even includes a rare unaged rye and a $110 23-year-old cask-strength Red Hook Rye, which was bottled exclusively for the store. But Tonya LeNell Smothers, the store's owner, isn't worried about other establishments stealing her rye customers. With supply so tight, "there's not a lot of rye to be had."

Rye fans can at last breathe a sigh of relief. The spirit is not likely to disappear from store shelves anytime soon. On the contrary, the rye fad is just getting started. In the next few years, as the spirit becomes easier to find in bars and stores, it should only increase in popularity. However, rye is still a niche product, and it will most likely always be one. But even though it may never sell as many cases as the more popular bourbon, rye is an important link to America's past that deserves preservation. And most important, it is good to have a bottle on hand for making cocktails. "You can't make an original Manhattan without rye," says Smothers.

he includes five recipes for different syrups, including one flavored with lemongrass and another flavored with lemon thyme. Readers can use these special syrups in the nine cocktails that Lieberman has included in his book.

The spirits themselves will also get spicier and more savory. Herb's Aromatic Infused Vodkas, first sold in 2006, are flavored with cilantro, rosemary, fennel, and dill. The vodka, developed by a couple of retired former Seagram's employees, sells for $29 a bottle. Russians have been infusing vodka with herbs for hundreds of years, but in America, the sweeter flavored vodkas have been much more popular. So far, Herb's is only available in certain markets, but by the end of 2007, distribution should be national. Jerome Hyafil, CEO of the Miami-based Garden Variety Vodka Company, which makes Herb's, believes that the spirit will be popular because it has a complex flavor. "We believe that herbs and infusions can deliver something closer to wine," Hyafil says. And just like wine, you can drink the vodka and even cook with it. Now's that's a savory drink.

CHAPTER SIX

Courtesy of Agua Luca

The New,
New Thing

. . . .

Around the world, distillers, marketers, and entrepreneurs are all struggling to solve a billion-dollar riddle: What's the next new drink of choice? With hundreds of vodkas, gins, and whiskies already on store shelves, there's little room and scant profits for upstarts. The real money is in finding an interesting spirit that's been overlooked or giving a tired spirit a premium makeover. No one was better at doing this than the late Sidney Frank, who turned the little-known German Jagermeister into a grassroots moneymaker and created the ultra-premium craze by producing the pricy Grey Goose vodka. Most of the companies trying to find the next new thing have used Frank's success as a blueprint, following his every move in hopes of getting the same result.

The game plan consists of a few essential elements. A spirit must have a catchy name and an untraditional, eye-catching bottle and label. The marketing plan generally needs to be two-pronged, taking advantage of traditional and grassroots resources. One of the keys to Grey Goose's success, which has been copied by most up-and-coming spirit manufacturers, is sponsoring parties and donating alcohol to different influential events and charities. (Grey Goose continues to use this strategy. It sponsors the Sundance Channel series *Iconoclasts,* which features celebrities interviewing each other, and summer polo matches in Bridgehampton, Long Island.) This technique could be called the trickle-down theory of marketing: If regular drinkers associate a certain brand with famous or wealthy people, then they will also order it in bars or buy bottles.

But for boutique spirits without large marketing budgets, there's still hope. Most often, these fledgling companies try to target a small number of very important customers. Usually this strategy involves sending emails to wealthy friends or friends of friends in hopes that they'll buy bottles in popular night clubs. What's even better is if the company can get a celebrity or a well-known socialite to drink the spirit. This can lead to a mention in the *New York Post*'s gossip column, "Page Six," or a gossip magazine like *Us Weekly.*

Cocktails are also becoming more important in the marketing of new spirits. A popular cocktail can drive sales of not just a brand but of an entire category. For example, the margarita sustained the tequila market in the United States for decades, and the martini craze of the late 1990s helped vodka to become even more popular. Many companies are also hiring mixologists to create cocktails in the hope that they'll catch on and become bar staples. Most spirit marketing campaigns now include several specially created drink recipes. Bacardi has a new campaign focusing on the mojito that tries to get consumers to associate the company's rum with the drink. It's reminiscent of Bacardi's efforts to become the liquor of choice for fixing a rum and Coke. Spirits giant Pernod Ricard, which owns a number of brands, including Wild Turkey, Beefeater Gin, and Stoli Vodka, has gone even further. In 2007, the company setup a "Spirits Desk" that creates themed or custom cocktails for journalists to include in their stories.

One reason for all this creative marketing is that spirits companies don't just have to woo drinkers but also restaurants, bars, and most importantly, distributors. Paradoxically, there must be great demand for a spirit or spirit category before a distributor will add it to its portfolio and really begin to push it. Like most investments, the most money usually gets made by those who get in on the ground floor. Often these are smaller companies and entrepreneurs who can invest time, often years, in carefully nurturing the growth of the spirit. This often is impossible for larger companies, which need a spirit to sell tens of thousands of cases immediately—but they can always acquire a smaller brand once it has taken off. "Big companies are just not good at building brands," says Gary Shansby, founder and chairperson of Partida Tequila. He's an expert on the topic—Shansby has spent most of his career building consumer brands, including Famous Amos Cookies and Terra Chips.

But big spirit companies are trying to get better at responding quickly to changes in consumer tastes. As a result, the rate of introductions of new spirits has sped up quite a bit over the last few years. Companies are also spending a lot more on test-marketing new products. For instance, before Diageo introduced its new Tanqueray Rangpur Gin, it tested the spirit for a whole summer in a number of southern mid-Atlantic states. The area was picked because it is quite diverse, so the company could get a sense of how different consumers would react to the new product. Salespeople for Diageo's distributor collected feedback from liquor store owners and bartenders. As a result, the company was able to tweak the gin and fine-tune its signature cocktail recipes.

Several years ago, most of the new products coming on the market were vodkas. But the "vodka [category] has become so cluttered," says Joe Bowman, cofounder of the new brand Agua Luca, which produces cachaca, the traditional Brazilian sugar cane rum. "Literally a new brand comes out every week." As a result, many of the industry's heavy hitters are exploring new spirit categories. Regardless of the category, most of the money is going toward starting high-end and super-premium brands. A new wave of potentially popular spirits, including tequila, rum, sake, and cachaca, are poised to take over the industry.

TEQUILA

As Gary Shansby travels around the world promoting his Partida tequila brand, people often wince when he takes out a bottle and starts pouring samples. "They remember a bad night," he says. And it's not just wicked hangovers that they associate with the spirit. Before a tasting begins, he usually has to clear up a few misconceptions about tequila: no, it's never bottled with a worm, and it's not made from cactus but from a plant that's a member of the lily family. Once he can actually get them to taste the tequila, they're pleasantly surprised that it is nothing like they remembered. "The biggest hurdle is educating consumers and bar staffs," he admits.

American's experience with tequila is usually pretty limited: either shots or margaritas. The spirit received some notoriety after the 1968 Olympics in Mexico City, but it was barely consumed in America until the mid 1970s. The margarita boom of the late 1970s helped increase the popularity of tequila for blender cocktails. And Jimmy Buffett's 1977 hit ballad "Margaritaville" made the cocktail a bar staple. But for the most part, the selection of tequila was very limited, and the majority was the unaged silver/blanco. Worse, much of the tequila imported into the United States was low quality, made from a cheaper blend of agave sugar and sugar cane.

Of course, in Mexico, tequila is regarded as the national drink, and there has always been a greater range of tequilas available, including higher-end spirits aged in oak barrels. (In fact, in Mexico, the least popular tequila is the *blanco*.) In the mid-1970s, the Mexican government declared that the spirit could only be made in one

So What Is Tequila?

Tequila is one of the most maligned and least understood spirits. And to set the record straight: no, it's never bottled with a worm.

Contrary to popular belief, tequila has a long and noble history that started centuries before it became a staple of fraternity parties. But up until a few years ago, it was hard to find anything but Jose Cuervo on liquor store shelves. Now the market is flooded with increasingly high-end tequilas. So what is tequila exactly?

Tequila's Origins

According to legend, hundreds of years ago, indigenous Mexicans living about two hours outside of Guadalajara only harvested the waxy leaves of the agave plant to use as a roofing material. (The leaves are waterproof.) Even though the plant looks like a cactus, the agave is really a member of the lily family. The Indians threw away the heart of the plant, known as "la piña" after its pineapple shape. One day, a bolt of lightning struck a pile of piñas and scorched them. The villagers realized that once baked, the agave plant would soften up and yield a sweet juice that could be fermented and turned into an alcoholic drink. For religious reasons, however, the villagers weren't allowed to get drunk off of the spirit. It was the Spanish colonizers who invaded Mexico in 1519 who began distilling this traditional brew to make the potent spirit tequila.

Since the creation of the spirit by the Spanish, its production methods have been refined. Dozens of varieties of agave grow in Mexico, but by law, tequila can now only be made from Blue Weber agave. (The plant is named after the German botanist who identified the variety.) It takes at least 8 and as many as 12 years to be

(continued)

mature enough for harvesting. A mature plant can stand up to 8 feet tall and 12 feet in circumference. Workers called *jimadors* use long-handled, razor-sharp, circular machetes, called *coas*, to trim the leaves of the plant and chop it down. The piñas on average weigh between 40 and 80 pounds but can be as heavy as 200 pounds. The trimmed piñas are then split and baked in an oven to convert the plant's starches into sugar. The piñas are then crushed, and the juice of the plant is collected, fermented, and finally distilled.

But since 1974, for a spirit to be considered "tequila," it has to be made in the Tequila region (just as sparkling wine made in California cannot be called Champagne)and must contain at least 51 percent agave juice. Spirits made outside this designated area or made from a different variety of agave are called mezcal, which is sometimes bottled with a worm. Mezcal has a richer, whiskylike taste because the piña isn't steamed but instead roasted and smoked. (When the sugar isn't all from agave, the spirit is called mixto. Most of the tequila sold in America is mixto.) Tequila is also smoother because it is usually distilled at least twice, whereas mezcal is usually only distilled once. Many of the tequila distilleries are in the state of Jalisco, while many mezcal producers are in Oaxaca.

Starting a few years ago, high-end tequila producers began advertising that their products are made exclusively from 100 percent blue agave. This difference was key in getting people to treat tequila as a premium spirit and pay premium prices. These marketing efforts were very similar to those used to promote single malt Scotch whisky.

Aging: *Blanco, Reposado, Añejo*

Most tequila brands offer at least three different varieties: *blanco* (a clear color), *reposado* (a gold color), and *añejo* (a bronze color).

These three categories reflect how long the spirit has been aged. The *blanco,* (also known as silver), best for margaritas, usually hasn't been aged at all. The *reposado* has been "rested" for between 60 days and a year in a wood barrel. And the *añejo,* best for sipping, has been aged for at least one year in oak. Just like Scotch or bourbon, the longer the tequila is aged, the more flavor it picks up from the barrel, and the darker it becomes. It's not uncommon for the *añejo* to have whiskylike notes.

area of the country and introduced some strict rules about how it could be produced.

The American perception of tequila completely changed in 1989 with the introduction of the premium brand Patrón. This tequila wasn't like any other on the market. The big difference is that the spirit is made from 100 percent blue agave. The decanter-like, hand-blown glass bottle (complete with cork stopper) was distinctive, not to mention the $40 price tag. The company's creation helped usher in a new, potentially lucrative category of spirits.

It was a risky move considering that tequila was, for the most part, a party spirit for college kids, and the idea of sipping it like a high-priced whisky seemed laughable. (To be fair, at the time, even single malt was just beginning to catch on.) Patrón was started by John Paul DeJoria and Martin Crowley. DeJoria knows a bit about starting companies; he's the cofounder and CEO of the John Paul Mitchell Systems hair care company, whose products are sold in roughly 90,000 American hair salons with annual retail sales of about $800 million. Even though DeJoria came from outside the spirits world, Patrón's success was closely followed by the rest of industry. At worst, the company's founders figured, if the spirit didn't sell, they would have plenty of holiday gifts for friends and family. But the gamble, of course, has more than paid off. Patrón now sells over a million cases each year. And from 1995 to 2005, overall sales of tequila, according to the Distilled Spirits Council of the United States (DISCUS), have almost doubled in the United States. According to Pernod Ricard, the super-premium tequila category has grown an estimated 25 percent over the last five years. High-priced tequila is no longer a joke. And Patrón has gone from being a lone innovator starting a new spirits category to the leader of a surging pack of high-priced tequilas.

In just the past five years, a flood of premium tequila brands has been created in or introduced to the United States. (Many of these fancy brands can be found only in America and aren't widely available in Mexico.) For instance, Gran Centenario, Jose Cuervo's brand of small-batch tequila, was introduced to the American market in 1996 but wasn't widely distributed until 2002. In 1995, the venerable Don Julio brand was finally introduced. Demand had been so strong for the brand's tequila that in the fall of 2006, the distillery was shut down for several months for a major renovation and expansion that will almost double the company's production. The 100 percent blue agave premium tequila Don Eduardo was created and introduced to the American market in 1998. And Shansby's brand, Partida, has only been around for a few years. He created the tequila with the Partida family, one of the largest agave growers in Mexico.

Spirit giants Bacardi and Pernod Ricard have also introduced premium tequila brands. In 2005, Bacardi introduced the super-hip Corzo tequila. The flasklike bottles were designed by Fabien Baron, who designed the bottle and advertising campaign for Calvin Klein's cK One perfume and Madonna's book *Sex*. The brand's *añejo* is particularly special, because after being distilled twice and resting in oak barrels for a couple of months, the spirit is distilled a third time.

Only the best of the distillate, the so-called "heart," is kept and aged again in barrels for over a year. This process allows the distiller to smooth out the tequila and pick up extra flavor from the barrels.

Months later, Pernod Ricard introduced Tezon. It, too, was packaged in a fashionable, nontraditional bottle that was inlaid with decorative symbols. Unlike many other premium tequilas on the market, the company uses an old-fashioned volcanic stone wheel to crush the baked agave and extract the plant's juices. In many other tequila plants, a large machine is used to juice the agave. Another key difference is that Tezon ferments the agave juice with the plant's fibers, instead of fermenting just the juice. Pernod Ricard claims these traditional techniques give the spirit a richer and more complex flavor.

Even Sidney Frank saw the potential in tequila. One of his last ventures before his death was Corazon tequila. (Reportedly, one stipulation of his sale of Grey Goose to Bacardi was that he couldn't immediately start a competing premium vodka or gin brand.) Just as with Grey Goose, at the heart of the advertising campaign for Corazon was branding: the spirit was touted as the "world's best-tasting tequila." Frank realized that, like vodka, there are quite a few premium tequilas, and one way to make his brand stand out to consumers was to put forth the idea that his spirit had been judged to taste better. It seemed as if his marketing magic worked. According to the beverage industry magazine *StateWays,* Corazon sold just 8,000 nine-liter cases in 2002 but was projected to sell 52,000 cases in 2005. That's an amazing 550 percent increase in just three years.

The spirit companies keep introducing ever more expensive tequila bottlings. The *añejos* that seemed pricey and exotic just a couple of years ago now seem like a relative bargain. One of the first was Jose Cuervo's Reserva de la Familia, which was introduced in 1995 for the company's 200th anniversary. Traditionally the tequila had just been, as the name suggests, given to the friends and family of the distillers. The Reserva sells for $100 and is bottled in a special hand-made glass bottle that is numbered and sealed in wax. Every year, the company has a Mexican artist design the tequila's box. Just six years after launching in the United States, Don Julio came out with two very special and pricey tequilas, 1942 ($125) and Real ($350).

One of the most interesting high-priced tequilas to come on the market is the limited-edition Leyenda ($250) from Gran Centenario, created in 2006. The tequila is the first spirit to get the new "Extra *Añejo*" classification from the Tequila Regulatory Council. This new category was created in March 2006 after years of discussion. To qualify for the new designation, a tequila has to be aged for a minimum of four years. Already several tequilas on the market qualify, but the Leyenda was the first to be certified. Like the other Gran Centenario tequilas, the Leyenda is aged in French Limousin oak casks, which give the spirit a nutty, cognaclike flavor. (French oak is usually used for wine, not spirit, casks.) Just as with single malt whisky, spirit connoisseurs are now increasingly interested in older tequilas and the type of cask used for the maturation. The quality of the agave is also becoming more important to drinkers.

Even Patrón, which started the ultra-premium trend, has created what it calls super-ultra-premium tequilas. In 2004, the company introduced a more expensive version of *blanco* called Gran Patrón Platinum that sells for about $200. The company's calls it "the world's finest platinum tequila." That's a big price tag and potentially a lot of profit, given that the company doesn't have to pay to age the spirit. But the tequila does come in a handmade crystal bottle and a curly maple wood box, both signed by the artists who created them. With so many tequilas selling for between $40 and $60, the original line of Patrón's tequilas no longer seemed as deluxe. "We wanted to expand the portfolio," says Matt Carroll, the vice president of marketing at Patrón. The Gran Patrón also allows the company to stay ahead of its competitors and "reinforces the company image." Even though Patrón didn't expect a huge demand for the pricey Platinum, in 2006, almost 40,000 bottles were sold.

To keep up with the industry's rising prices, in spring 2007, Patrón came out with an even more expensive small-batch tequila called Gran Patrón Burdeos, which sells for $500. The special spirit, which is limited to a few hundred cases, is aged in Bordeaux casks. Even though finishing single malt whisky in wine casks is quite popular and common, this idea is revolutionary for the tequila industry. Tequila is usually aged in former bourbon or French oak casks. If the Gran Patrón Burdeos is popular, it could potentially lead to a whole new category of tequilas finished in different types of wood.

According to tequila companies, over the last three or four years, the spirit has really taken off, and keeping up with demand has been a challenge. The spirit's popularity has even helped cause a recent agave shortage. But tequila isn't only popular in bars and liquor stores. Hotels, restaurants, and even spas have begun to offer tequila-themed dinners and promotions. In 2006, Patrón and the upscale chain of Mexican restaurants, Rosa Mexicano, offered a special five-course Day of the Dead dinner at a number of its locations around the country. The JW Marriott Starr Pass Resort & Spa in Tucson, Arizona, has a nightly tequila toast for guests. And the resort's lobby lounge also stocks over 150 different tequilas, including some that the bar has infused. The Fairmont San José partnered with El Tesoro for a special $85-per-plate dinner at the beginning of 2006. The owner and master distiller of the tequila company Carlos Camarena was there to sign bottles and greet the guests.

You don't even have to drink tequila to enjoy the spirit. A number of Four Seasons hotels have offered a detoxifying massage that uses a rub made from tequila and sage oil. But the resort that has arguably gone the farthest is the CasaMagna Marriott in Puerto Vallarta, Mexico, which not only has a tequila sommelier but grows its own agave on site, which it uses to make a house brand of tequila.

The major spirits companies are betting heavily that the tequila category will continue to grow. But unlike vodka, the ante to get into the tequila game is a little steeper. Premium tequila is made only from 100 percent agave, which takes about a decade to fully mature. Plus, the *añejos* and the *reposados* need to be aged, which isn't cheap. Nevertheless, Shansby predicts that over the next ten years, sales of the category will triple with the super-premium offerings leading the way. And tequila has been fortunate in that many celebrities and tastemakers have championed the spirit, leading to particularly high sales in high-end bars and clubs. Companies have also wisely packaged their products in eye-catching and unusual ways.

But unlike premium vodka, *añejo* and *reposado* tequila are hard to use in cocktails. Even for professional bartenders, using the spirit in mixed drinks can be a challenge, although the margarita continues to be extremely popular. This might ultimately limit the growth of this category unless people are willing to sip the older tequilas like whisky or pay even more for the unaged spirit.

SAKE

Walk into almost any New York City grocery store, and you're likely to find freshly made sushi rolls, sashimi, and even steamed edamame. But this isn't just a big-city phenomenon. Across the country, Japanese food has gone from exotic treat to mundane meal found in shopping mall food courts. And sushi has entered into the pantheon of foreign foods—like fajitas, bagels, and spaghetti—that are now staples of the modern American diet. How big has Japanese food become? Thanks to the *Iron Chef* television series, one time Nobu chef Morimoto is now practically a household name; he runs a number of restaurants in the United States and even has his own line of knives and beer.

Sake, the Japanese alcohol made from fermented rice, has also recently become more popular. (Sake has actually been available in the United States since the late 1860s, but until recently, very little was consumed.) In 2005, sake imports grew by an impressive 18 percent. (However, experts partially chalk up that increase to sake importers getting a bit too excited and bringing in too many bottles.) Overall consumption, according to Chris Pearce, a sake expert and president of World Sake Imports, should double every seven years. "Sake is not a trend," he says. "Sake will continue this consistent steady growth." The selection of sakes available in America has grown, and some of the better small-batch sakes are finally being imported. "I'm always trying something new," says Roger Dagorn, master sommelier at the downtown New York institution Chanterelle. On any given night, between 8 and 20 sakes are on his wine list. The restaurant has also been holding an extremely popular sake dinner annually since 1999. Each of the meal's courses is paired with a very fine artisanal sake. What makes the night even more special is that a number of the sake makers usually attend the dinner.

Since 2001, a huge tasting called the "Joy of Sake" organized by Pearce has exposed thousands of Americans to some of the finest sakes. Originally the event took place in Honolulu, but it has now expanded to San Francisco and New York. In 2006, the three tastings attracted about 2,700 people who had 299 sakes to sample.

Unfortunately, most Americans have only tried warm sake—if they've tasted it at all. Even though warm sake can be great on a cold night, usually only lower-grade commercial sake is heated. The best sakes are supposed to be served cold. (Heat can dull the flavor.) In Japan, according to Pearce, between 1,200 and 1,300 sake brewers produce about 10,000 different sakes. Only about 350 or 400 of these brands are available in the United States. And worse, "a lot of them you never see anywhere," says Pearce. But that's slowly changing as more higher-quality sakes become available in this country.

One problem, however, is that sake doesn't travel all that well, making importation a little more complicated. Ideally sake, like wine, should be shipped in refrigerated containers.

But the sake selection in the United States will likely increase as American consumption continues to grow. This is particularly good news for sake producers, because consumption of the alcohol is actually declining in Japan. "Japanese consumers have become more wine drinkers than sake drinkers," says Chanterelle's Dagorn. As a result, the number of sake producers in Japan has actually decreased during the last few years.

Most experts agree that younger American drinkers are driving this increase in sake consumption. They have grown up eating sushi and enjoying Japanese cultural imports, like Nintendo video games, anime movies, and Pokémon trading cards. And many hip bars are using the alcohol in cocktails, including the popular saketini. Sake sales will continue to increase as long as the better handcrafted sakes become more widely available in this country.

RUM

Dark rum drinkers have never gone thirsty. There has always been a big selection of aged and expensive rums from all over the Caribbean. One reason is that the spirit was the drink of choice for sailors, and for years it fortified the British navy. Yet if you like white rum, until recently, you really didn't have much to choose from—basically Bacardi.

But the spirits industry has high hopes for the rum category, especially for premium white rum brands. The spirit has always been popular, but it has the potential of being as popular as vodka. Both spirits are easily mixed in drinks, but because rum has more flavor, it can also be sipped. As a result, a number of new, high-end, premium white rums are now trying to compete with premium vodkas.

Ten years ago, premium white rum might have been a tough sell, but the rum category is booming, encouraging small entrepreneurs and spirit giants both to start new light rum brands. According to DISCUS, since 1990, the overall rum category has grown an amazing 61 percent and, in 2005, over 20 million nine-liter cases were sold. Traditionally rum hasn't been thought of as a premium spirit in this country. "People associate rum with drinks that have umbrellas," admits Jeffrey Zarnow, the chairman and CEO of the new Starr African Rum. Even today, one of the most popular cocktails is the simple Cuba libre, also known as rum and Coke. But that's changing with the recent popularity of rum-based pre-Prohibition cocktails and the mojito fad. The mojito used to be a summer cocktail, but it's so popular, it has now turned into a bar staple served year-round. "The mojito has become the new cosmo," says Zarnow.

This category of pricy light rums is just a few years old. One of the first premium white rums to hit shelves was Zarnow's Starr African Rum from Mauritius, introduced in October 2004. Before he started the company, Zarnow was running a film production firm in Hollywood. A friend tasted the rum on a trip to Africa and asked Zarnow to help him import it to the United States. Zarnow liquidated his assets and put another $100,000 on his credit cards to get the company off the ground. He even designed the brand's unique deep red, pyramid-shaped bottle. (Zarnow had a pretty good idea of what the bottle should look like, and the company couldn't afford the $85,000 that a professional bottle designer wanted to do the job. "All my gray hairs come from that bottle design," he says.) Zarnow admits that when he started the company, he didn't really know much about the spirits business or even how the rum was made. What he did know was how the spirit tasted. "I was blown away," he says. Starr African is a blend of a couple of different rums, some as old as six years, which makes for a very smooth spirit.

But when Zarnow started approaching bars and distributors, it wasn't easy to convince them to stock his $35 rum. It was just as hard to convince them that there was a demand for high-end rums at all. So he decided to target the drinker before trying to sell the spirit. One tactic the brand has used successfully is getting celebrities to drink the spirit. On the company's website, you can read blurbs from such celebrity magazines as *People* and *Us Weekly* about how Tom Cruise, Snoop Dogg, and Leonardo DiCaprio have been seen drinking the rum. The resulting buzz surrounding the spirit has hopefully made it easier to get the rum onto store shelves and into bars. "You build a brand one drinker at a time," he says. "This isn't a race but a marathon."

What helped Zarnow convince people of the legitimacy of premium rum was the launch of 10 Cane Rum by heavyweight Moet Hennessy and Oronoco by Diageo. 10 Cane was introduced in 2005 after seven years of development. "It was the first time Moet Hennessy created a brand from scratch," says Stephanie Chassing, the brand manager for the rum. "It was a big leap of faith." The company put together a team to develop 10 Cane, creating an almost boutique company within the Moet Hennessy corporate structure. The company wanted to use all its resources and centuries of experience to "try to create the best rum," says Chassing.

The company's press release about the launch of the spirit hammered home this point. It declared 10 Cane to be "the first brand which promises to bring luxury, style, and innovation to the long-neglected rum category. This is rum's redemption." The release goes on to warn drinkers that this spirit shouldn't be confused with the rum enjoyed by beach vacationers or college kids on spring break. The company clearly wanted the spirit to set the standard for the whole premium rum category. And it's priced accordingly. Just like Starr and Oronoco, the rum usually retails at or above $35, which makes these new rums even more expensive than Grey Goose, Ketel One, and the other premium vodkas.

10 Cane is made in Trinidad from hand-harvested sugarcane that is pressed the same day it's cut. (The rum is very similar to the Brazilian cachaca. Both are made from sugar cane juice instead of from molasses, like many other rums. You'll read more about cachaca, Brazil's national drink, in the next section.) And just as if making an extra virgin olive oil, the company only gently presses the cane once, extracting about 75 percent of the stalk's juice. The process is relatively expensive, but the result is a more concentrated juice that contains none of the cane's bitterness. "You don't want to keep everything because you would have too many impurities," Chassing explains. What makes the pressing particularly challenging is that the cane is very fragile—even more fragile than wine grapes. After being fermented, the juice is distilled twice in a small, onion-shaped still, and then it rests in barrels made from French oak. It's then packaged in a distinctive bottle with a very long neck, which is supposedly easier for bartenders to grab while making drinks.

Oronoco was introduced just a few months after 10 Cane in the fall of 2005. The rum comes in a unique, hand-labeled, batch-numbered cylindrical bottle. The way the rum is made is also unique. To create the spirit, Diageo worked with Roberto and Vicente Bastos Ribeiro, who made their name creating cachaca. Oronoco is a blend of Brazilian sugarcane rum (cachaca, essentially) and a little bit of South American rum. The cane is hand harvested in the mountains and almost immediately crushed. The cane juice is then fermented and distilled three times. The cachaca and the South American rum are then married together in a cask made from Brazilian Amendoim wood. This unusual production method ensures that the rum is unlike any other on the market.

A lot of money is being invested in developing and marketing these three new white rums and this new premium category. One reason for the expenditure is that the learning curve is so steep for consumers. "No one knows the qualities of selecting a good rum," says 10 Cane's Chassing. Because the category is so new, unlike Scotch whisky, consumers aren't sure why they should pay for a premium rum. As a result, tastings are particularly important for these brands. "We're really into creating the emotional link between the brand and the consumer," says Chassing.

It's too early to say whether or not premium rum will catch on. And since these brands were introduced, a number of other premium white and dark rums have come on the market. One of the new brands is Bambu White Rum, launched in the winter of 2005. The company claims it's extra smooth because it is filtered four times and distilled three times. Even Patrón, the tequila giant, has a line of aged rums just in case the category really takes off. Who knows? Maybe lightning will strike twice.

CACHACA

Over the last five years, Brazil and Brazilian culture has become extremely popular with young people in the United States. It's possible that the country hasn't garnered this much popular attention since the late 1950s and early 1960s, when the movie *Black Orpheus* was released and Stan Getz and João and Astrud Gilberto recorded the hit song "The Girl From Ipanema." In 2005, almost 800,000 Americans visited the country, up almost 20 percent from 2003. Brazil has become so hip, it's been paid the ultimate compliment, serving as the backdrop for a number of popular music videos, including one from Snoop Dogg and Pharrell Williams. The country has also served as the setting for a number of TV shows, including an MTV reality series. And not only the small screen has fallen for South America's largest country; a museum exhibit about the country's Tropicália movement toured the United States in 2006. Speaking of works of art, it doesn't hurt that the country is also the home of supermodel Gisele Bündchen.

Perhaps the one Brazilian cultural icon that hasn't yet caught on in the States is the national drink: cachaca. The spirit is a type of rum made from fermented sugar cane juice. Most of the rums from the Caribbean aren't made directly from cane sugar but molasses, a by-product of the refinement of sugar. Brazilians have been making the spirit for hundreds of years, and it's popular across Latin America, Asia, and Europe. In Brazil, there are 5,000 brands of cachaca, and about 1.5 billion liters are sold every year. Overall consumption of cachaca worldwide is so large, it trails behind only vodka and the Asian favorite, soju. But the spirit has never really caught on with Americans. "No one has cracked the code," says Bowman, cofounder of Agua Luca. What little cachaca was imported languished in obscurity at the back of store shelves while the rest of the white spirits category took off. But a number of spirits companies are trying to change that with the introduction of new premium cachaca brands.

The potential is huge for the spirit because it's versatile and has the benefit of being tied to Brazil. And cachaca even has its own delicious signature cocktail: the caipirinha. The drink is a mixture of cachaca, muddled limes, sugar, and ice. Many bars in America already have it on their menus, though vodka or rum is often substituted for cachaca because the spirit can still be hard to find and, until recently, could be much harsher than the substitute liquor. A few years ago, there would have been slim hope for an unknown, foreign-sounding, labor-intensive cocktail. But the widespread success of the mojito has changed the industry's conventional thinking, and because the recipe for the caipirinha is very similar to that of the mojito, selling the drink to consumers should be easier. One company, Excalibur Enterprise, has such high hopes for the cocktail that it sells a premade version called the Beleza Pura Caipirinha. Company founder Olie Berlic needed over four years to develop the ideal recipe for the drink.

Interestingly enough, the premium cachacas that are flooding the American market aren't well established Brazilian brands but were created by American entrepreneurs. (That might change soon. Supposedly some of the largest Brazilian spirit companies are contemplating entering the American market.) Most of these upstart companies share very similar stories. Usually the brand's founder was in some other kind of business and stumbled upon cachaca on a visit to Brazil. After tasting the spirit and seeing how popular it is in Brazil, the entrepreneur decided to partner with a local producer to create a line of premium cachaca for Americans. Although these brands are relatively new, you wouldn't know it from looking at the bottles. Most of the cachacas are slickly packaged and don't look out of place behind a fancy bar next to established premium spirits. That's no accident. One company, Agua Luca, hired a French design firm that has worked with Grey Goose, Ketel One, and Veuve Clicquot to create its packaging. The result: a distinctive cylindrical-shaped bottle. Beleza Pura hired the legendary commercial designer Milton Glaser to redo its logo and bottles.

What's inside these stylish bottles is also quite premium. To compete against expensive vodkas, gins, and tequilas, the cachaca has to be extra smooth but also have a complex flavor. To achieve a high level of quality, these companies have had to use only the best production methods or even introduce new techniques. For example, many of these companies only use the sweeter heart of the sugarcane stalk. Even though the top and bottom of the plant contain sugar and can be used, they contain more astringent flavors.

Many of the brands insist on handpicking the sugarcane to make sure it is mature and ripe. Many larger Brazilian companies will harvest a whole field at once, which is easier but also means you get some cane that isn't ready to be picked. Traditionally, a whole field of cane is set on fire, which speeds up the harvesting. Mae de Ouro, which was started by a researcher at an investment bank and debuted during the summer of 2004, is not only against fire harvesting but exclusively uses cane that has been grown in an environmentally responsible way. Some companies only use fresh-cut sugarcane and immediately crush it. This small change limits the bitterness in the sugar and in the resulting spirit.

Many of these new cachacas are distilled and filtered multiple times, and the heart of the distillate that is bottled is quite small. Generally distillers don't bottle the spirit that comes out of the still at the beginning and at the end. The premium spirit makers throw away more of these so-called "heads" and "tails." Even though this process is more expensive, it makes the spirit smoother and prevents some of the most bitter elements from getting into the alcohol. Leblon cachaca goes even further to ensure smoothness. The spirit is aged in old cognac casks and bottled in Cognac, France. According to Steve Luttman, Leblon's president, the company is "approaching it like [making] an Eau de Vie."

It is hard to say if cachaca will ever catch on in the United States. A boom is at least five or ten years away. It's going to take a while to educate consumers, bartenders, and distributors about the spirit and how it can be used. But the spirit has already come a long way. "This has been a labor of love," says Olie Berlic, who claims to have introduced the first premium handcrafted cachacas to the American market. "I was turned down I don't know how many times." Clearly it's not as hard now to get a cachaca brand off the ground, given the number of brands competing for space on store shelves. But at this point, the more the merrier. "We're happy to see other brands out there," says Bowman. "It increases the pie." The cumulative effect of all this marketing should get attention for the category. Cachaca could also really take off if the caipirinha suddenly becomes as popular as the mojito. Then the question will be, what brand do you want used in your cocktail?

Cognac: The Spirit of Kings

Cognac, the noble spirit, has always been the drink of kings, from Napoleon to Queen Elizabeth. And now it's the drink of choice of a new set of royalty: the kings of hip-hop, from Jay-Z to P. Diddy to Busta Rhymes. Just like fancy cars and diamond-encrusted jewelry, expensive cognac has become one of the requisite trappings of young celebrities. In just a few years, cognac has undergone a major face-lift to become the perfect party spirit. And thanks to this patronage, over the last ten years, the demand for cognac has spiked. According to DISCUS, sales of nine-liter cases of cognac were projected to grow by 20 percent between 2002 and 2006.

This increase in American cognac sales couldn't have come at a better time. For years, one of the spirit's best customers was Japan, but that country's economic decline and the recent surge in popularity of vintage French wine and white spirits has caused Japanese sales of cognac to drop drastically. According to a report produced for the 2006 Vinexpo Asia-Pacific conference, brandy sales in Japan were down by almost 54 percent from 1999 to 2004. The report forecasted that sales would continue to decrease. But a bright spot is China, which has a growing appetite for cognac and is projected to be a major market for it in the near future.

The history of cognac has been marked by many such fluctuations. The spirit was first developed hundreds of years ago when merchants were trying to find a way to ship French wine to customers in Holland without its spoiling. It was discovered that distilling the wine extended its life significantly. Another benefit was that the resulting spirit was more concentrated, making it much easier to transport. Before long, people discovered that the cognac benefited from maturing in the oak barrels in which it was shipped.

Much of the spirit's flavor and the color comes from the wood barrels. Today the spirit can only be made in southwest France in the Cognac region. (If the spirit is made elsewhere, it is simply called brandy.) Cognac is made from just a few different grape varietals and is distilled twice in an copper pot still before being aged in French oak casks.

The height of cognac's popularity was actually in the 1800s. It took a worldwide agriculture disaster to derail its success. An epidemic of phylloxera , an aphidlike insect, destroyed grape vines across the continent. As a result, cognac production ceased for several years until a disease-resistant root stock could be found. In those years, drinkers discovered other spirits, and cognac was never to able to achieve its former dominance.

The recent popularity of cognac in the United States can be traced to the late 1990s, when young people discovered the spirit. A breakthrough moment happened when Courvoisier approached Russell Simmons, founder of Def Jam Recordings and the Phat Farm clothing company, to help market the spirit in America. Cognac has always been popular with African Americans, but once the Busta Rhymes and P. Diddy song "Pass the Courvoisier" hit airways, sales increased overnight. According to a *BusinessWeek* profile of Simmons, sales of Courvoisier increased by 20 percent in 2002. Courvoisier has embraced this new demographic and even sponsored the official after-party of the 2006 BET hip-hop awards in Atlanta.

But not only Courvoisier has gotten the attention of rappers. Jay-Z, the current president and CEO of Def Jam Recordings, also owns the chain of 40/40 Clubs. The New York location has a number of private party rooms, and one, called the "Cognac Room," has a

(continued)

selection of expensive bottles from different houses. There's also the "Remy Lounge," dedicated to Jay-Z's favorite cognac house.

Despite its regal air, cognac is trying to become more accessible to everyday drinkers and capitalize on its popularity with younger consumers. The various houses have tried a number of different strategies, from covering New York City subway cars with splashy ads to introducing redesigned logos and untraditional packaging. One striking example is Landy Cognac's Desir, sold in a bottle in the shape of a curvaceous woman. The bottle is covered in a slinky red dress and has a wide-brimmed red hat. Francis Abecassis has gone even further, naming one of its cognac lines ABK6. The name is derived from the house's name and is spelled as if it were a quick text message on a cell phone. The cognac also comes in an untraditional squat bottle with a very small label. The company says the bottle is going after urban, style-conscious consumers and is meant to compete with premium vodka.

To get the attention of so-called "metrosexuals" and other stylish men, Hennessy has published a book called *Manifest X.O: Style Fundamentals for the Good Life.* Each of the guide's 12 chapters is dedicated to a different topic, including wine and spirits, sex, and even "gentleman's etiquette." The book is an attempt by Hennessy to get drinkers to link the company's premium XO spirit to the "good life."

In an effort to appeal to a wider audience, some companies are actually trying to make cognac easier to drink. The best way to do this is to flavor the spirit or blend it with juice or a sweetener. This obviously isn't a new concept. "Everything certainly comes around," says Larry Kass, spokesperson for the family-owned spirits giant Heaven Hill. Grand Marnier, a blend of cognac and orange essence, has been on the market since 1880. Pineau des

Charentes, a mixture of grape juice and cognac, is a traditional drink of the Cognac region. But over the last few years, a number of new cognac blends have been introduced. During 2004, Grand Marnier introduced a vanilla-flavored, cognac-based spirit called Navan. Not only is the flavoring different than that of traditional Grand Marnier, but it's packaged in a clear, updated version of the company's signature squat bottle.

Arguably the first of these new cognac products was Alize, introduced by Kobrand in 1986. The original Alize is a mix of cognac and a number of juices, including passion fruit. The brand wasn't an immediate hit, but by the 1990s, younger and more urban drinkers had discovered the spirit. It even found its way into a number of rap songs. The brand has now grown to include several flavors, and a few years ago Kobrand even introduced a line of traditional cognacs. Then in 2001, an entrepreneur launched Hpnotiq, a blend of cognac, vodka, and fruit juice (it was acquired in 2003 by Heaven Hill),. Not only is this mixture unique, but the spirit is also a distinctive color: baby blue. The spirit has gotten a lot of media attention and has been marketed as the drink of choice of celebrities, especially rappers.

The famous cognac houses have also started producing blends. In 1998, Rémy Martin introduced a line of cognac blends called Rémy Red, which includes a red berry infusion, a strawberry kiwi infusion, and a grape berry infusion. According to the company, these Rémy Red products have just "a touch of Rémy Martin cognac."

The cognac houses are also pushing ever more expensive limited-edition bottles. These high-end offerings have always been the specialty of the region, but with more celebrities and high-rollers drinking cognac, an increasing number of houses are selling extra-

(continued)

old and special bottles. In fact, according to DISCUS, sales of the lower-priced VS have been growing slowly while sales of the more expensive VSOP and XO are surging. Between 2002 and 2006, XO sales increased by over 86 percent, and sales of VSOP increased by over 40 percent. One of the rarest cognacs on the market today is the Rémy Martin Louis XIII, which sells for over $1,300 and contains eau-de-vie that is 100 years old. The cognac comes in a handblown Baccarat crystal decanter that has a 24-karat gold collar, a design based on a decanter from the 1500s that was found near the Rémy Martin estate. For serious cognac aficionados, every few years Rémy produces a limited-edition Louis XIII bottling. In 2007, the company released 786 bottles of Louis XIII Black Pearl, which each sold for $8,000. The special Baccarat decanter is made from black crystal and has platinum accents. The company sent out notices to select customers, inviting them to buy a bottle before the vintage went on sale to the general public.

Cognac houses have also dug deep into their storehouses to pull out rare aged spirits. Just like champagne, once every few years, the quality of the grapes and the resulting cognac is particularly exquisite. This cognac is put aside and stored separately from the rest of a house's inventory. For instance, last year, Cognac Ferrand released 600 bottles of a very rare 1914 cognac, which sells for $1,000. The spirit was made in a wood-fired alembic pot still and was stored for 75 years in French oak barrels. (The cognac was then moved to glass demijohns.) The 1914 vintage is particularly sought-after by cognac drinkers and collectors. The year 1914 is often referred to as "the Year of the Lady" because the vintage was made by women while the men of Cognac were away fighting the Germans in World War I. As a result, according to Ferrand, the cognac has a lighter flavor and is particularly elegant.

Vintage cognacs have become the signature of Hine, which releases a few of these special spirits each year. In 2005, for example, the house released a 1957 ($500), a 1975 ($350), a 1981($300), and a 1983 ($285). Over the last few years, as demand has grown, America has gotten an increasingly large allocation of Hine's very limited and expensive cognacs.

Cognac companies are also trying to move away from the idea that cognac can be sipped only from a crystal snifter. Historically, the spirit was used in cocktails, most famously in the sidecar and the brandy Alexander. But after World War II, the cocktail culture began to disappear, and the great cognac drinks slowly faded into obscurity. However, with the recent rebirth of the cocktail culture, bartenders are again using cognac in their mixed drinks. And the cognac houses couldn't be happier. Rémy Martin is even actively pushing the mixability of its cognac. It has developed several drink recipes, including one called the Rémy Dragon, a combination of the company's VSOP and a number of ingredients, including mango juice, mashed ginger, Grenadine, and even a splash of Sprite soda. Landy Cognac, part of Cognac Ferrand, has developed an even more irreverent cocktail—the French orgasm. The drink calls for Landy XO, cranberry juice, lemon juice, and Mathilde Raspberry. This is certainly not your grandfather's drink!

CHAPTER SEVEN

Courtesy of Agua Luca

Last Call

· · · · · · · ·

IF YOU'VE READ this far, then you know that spirits have definitely come a long way in the last few years. Because of a confluence of different trends, the industry has enjoyed a veritable golden age since the late 1990s. It's also not a bad time to be a drinker. After years in the shadow of beer and wine, liquor has finally regained the limelight. Historically the spirits business has been cyclical, marked by booms and busts in popularity. Clearly we're now in the midst of one of these booms.

Even during the writing of this book, it has been hard to keep up with the rapid introduction of new and interesting spirits. To capitalize on the popularity of drinks, distillers are trying to increase production as much as they can. Some of the most successful Scottish single malt whisky companies, like Macallan, have reached maximum capacity. They are now running their distilleries 24 hours a day, 7 days a week, and still have trouble meeting demand. That's partly due to the phenomenal growth of the global spirits market. Master distillers spend more time than ever traveling around the world to visit customers. Jimmy Russell, master distiller of Wild

Turkey, now routinely visits customers as far away as Japan and Australia. No doubt China will soon be added to distillers' itineraries if it's not already a stop. Just as with oil and steel, the country will soon buy an increasingly greater share of the world's spirits production.

Spirit manufacturers are also trying to devise new ways to make their products ever more "premium." What seemed pricey or expensive a few years ago now seems like a deal. In many conversations, experts and company executives say that brands feel the need to make their products more expensive to create buzz and attract more customers. The question that many spirits companies are now struggling with is how premium will they go? Beefeater gin, always considered a premium product, now doesn't seem all that expensive at a mere $20 a bottle. The company is working to create an ultra-premium gin and is deciding how high to price it. Beefeater is even considering one option that would ultimately cost consumers around $100. That's a huge leap for the gin category, considering that Tanqueray No. Ten, currently the most expensive mass-market gin, sells for less than half that price.

One reason this question is particularly vexing for large spirit companies is that they face increasing competition from unlikely sources. Everyone, from microbreweries to celebrities to restaurants, seems to be producing spirits. In March 2005, the New York restaurant Aquavit appropriately introduced its own line of white cranberry-infused aquavit. The Scandinavian restaurant had been making and serving its own infusions for years, but customers weren't able to purchase bottles of these special spirits. Working with a distiller in Sweden, the restaurant infuses Swedish grain alcohol with Massachusetts cranberries. The aquavit sells for nearly $30 a bottle and is available only in the New York City area, although the restaurant is exploring greater distribution. The restaurant has since added its own line of champagne made by a small French producer. The signature bubbly is available only in the restaurant and sells for $16 a glass and $65 a bottle.

Billionaire entrepreneur Richard Branson has gone even further. In 1994, he founded Virgin Drinks, whose first product was an eponymous line of cola. Branson has branched out and now produces his own line of ice tea, juice, energy drinks, wine, and now a vodka called, of course, Virgin Vodka. The triple-distilled spirit is sold on Virgin Atlantic flights for about $20. It's not hard to imagine that other restaurants, bars, clubs, airlines, or hotels will soon launch or brand their own lines of alcohol.

But sustaining the present popularity of spirits will definitely be a challenge for the industry. With an increasing array of bottles flooding the market, manufacturers run the risk of overwhelming consumers and losing their momentum. Pricing is also tricky. If prices are too low, consumers won't think a product is deluxe or even good. But if prices are too high, they may become alienated and feel taken advantage of. At the same time, many companies with high-priced spirits are concerned that their products soon will be leapfrogged by other, even more expensive brands, stealing their attention and market share.

Not all companies are playing exclusively to the high end. Some industry experts predict that the next wave of popular spirits will look like luxury products but carry value price tags. For these to be successful, consumers must feel they're getting a great drink without downgrading. They need to feel savvy and not embarrassed to bring a bottle to a party. The Australian Yellow Tail wine has successfully marketed itself this way. But the most successful use of this strategy is the airline JetBlue, which is known as much for its luxury leather seats and satellite TV as for low fares.

Skyy Vodka is one of the first spirits to successfully promote itself this way. The domestically produced vodka sells for between $15 to $20, half as much as the fancier imported vodkas on the market. The company's website states: "In essence, paying more ensures a fancier bottle, but not necessarily higher quality vodka." Consumers can justify buying the vodka, even if it has a lower price tag, thanks to Skyy's claim that its product contains fewer impurities than the competition because it is quadruple distilled and filtered three times. The company backs this up with statistics from an independent lab. The vodka is also packed in a hip, expensive-looking blue bottle.

The marketing campaign has worked. During the last 13 years, the number of bottles that Skyy has sold has increased by double-digit percentages. (For those intent on buying premium vodka, in March 2005, the company introduced Skyy 90, which retails for about $35. It took the company 10 years and $25 million to develop this luxury product.)

Over the next few years, no doubt other big spirit brands will follow Skyy's lead. In addition, as prices for spirits climb, consumers looking for bargains will do more of their alcohol shopping in supermarkets and warehouse clubs. These big retailers are also trying to make this a reality. According to a story in *The Wall Street Journal* in 2005, Wal-Mart is working with spirits giant Diageo to boost alcohol sales from about a $1 billion a year to $5 billion by 2010. The plan is particularly ironic, because Wal-Mart's headquarters is in a dry county of Arkansas, where liquor is not sold, and according to the *Journal*'s story, the company bans alcohol at all corporate functions. Not only can these big chain retailers offer discounts that small liquor stores can't match, but they are now coming out with their own lines of spirits. It's not a new idea; across Europe, many supermarkets already have their own lines of value spirits, but the trend has taken a while to reach America.

In the fall of 2006, Costco introduced Kirkland Signature Vodka, part of its house brand of products. The supposed ultra-premium, small-batch vodka is made in Cognac, France, from wheat and is distilled five times and filtered twice. The production process, according to the company, "makes it among the smoothest vodkas available on the market today." The vodka, packaged in a fancy clear bottle, doesn't look like a house brand, and you wouldn't know that it came from Costco unless you were familiar with the Kirkland brand name. The vodka is also a bargain. For $30 you get 1.75 liters. A comparable size of Grey Goose sells for about $50 at Costco stores. "It seemed like a natural fit and proved successful," says Annette Alvarez-Peters, Costco's assistant general-merchandise manager of the wine, spirits, and beer program. It was even more successful than the company expected, and the vodka was actually sold out for a while.

Costco also purchased a barrel of Scottish whisky made by Macallan from a private bottler. In November 2006, the retailer started selling the 19-year-old single malt for $70. It is labeled with both the Macallan and Kirkland name. It's a good deal, considering that the 21-year-old Fine Oak Macallan sells for about $220. Costco hasn't announced any other spirits offerings but is supposedly working on expanding the Kirkland line.

Private label spirits is a logical step, because many of these stores, including Albertsons and Whole Foods, already have introduced their own lines of wines. Alvarez-Peters says, in fact, that the popularity of Costco's wine led the company to develop its signature vodka. Some of these wines, like Trader Joe's fantastically popular Two Buck Chuck, are intended to target the lower end of the market, while some, including Costco's, are intended to compete against premium wines from the best regions around the world. According to the Private Label Manufacturers Association, in 2006, U.S. supermarkets sold $2 billion worth of spirits, and just over 5 percent of that was private label. Over the next few years, no doubt that percentage will grow as spirit house brands become more commonplace.

In the not-too-distant future, bars and lounges are likely to rethink their prices. Consumers may seem willing to pay $12, $14, or $16 for a well-mixed cocktail. As traditional cocktails become increasingly available around the country, and even in the air, many more people will begin to trade up and order them. But prices can't really get any higher over the next few years without losing customers.

Few establishments in the country could sell enough $20 cocktails to stay open. The industry has to realize that these fancy cocktails are still the exception and, for many people, only an occasional treat. A whisky drinker may pull out a cherished bottle of expensive single malt for special occasions but will pour a less expensive blended whisky for a regular drink.

The art of the cocktail was almost lost, but now under the stewardship of a new generation of talented mixologists, it will hopefully flourish at all price levels. To ensure that happens, bartenders must continue to offer traditional drinks as well as new and enticing creations that feature popular flavors and ingredients.

The spirits industry also must evolve with and take advantage of changes in consumer tastes. This process may take time. Just as in the hotel business, a major change made today by a whisky company won't take effect for years down the road. Over the last few years, this tortoiselike pace hasn't been a big problem, because demand has been so great, rewarding most decisions. But as people get used to drinking spirits and cocktails again and perhaps a new trend sweeps across the nation, the industry will definitely need to become more nimble. The good news is that laws regarding alcohol sales are becoming more liberal. This should allow manufacturers to respond more quickly to consumer behavior. Plus many innovators and entrepreneurs are working to continually reinvent and propel the spirits business.

When I started working on this book, I was aware that a number of spirits trends had helped increase sales and revitalize the industry. But what I didn't realize was just how many different trends there are and how they continually develop. Hopefully I've been able to cover the most important ones in this book. Surely, I couldn't have chosen a better period in which to examine the growth of this fascinating industry.

Acknowledgments

. . . .

FOR YEARS, IT had been a dream of mine to write a book on spirits, but it was my agent, Farley Chase, who made this a reality. He believed in and has been excited about the project since our first meeting. His unflagging support was invaluable to me throughout this whole process.

My editor at Kaplan, Joshua Martino, was also instrumental in shepherding the manuscript into an actual book. His sincere interest in the topic and in the project was more than any writer could hope for.

During the course of writing this book, I interviewed countless experts in the spirits and cocktails business. I will always be grateful to them for their generosity and willingness to answer my every last question. These fascinating people are what make the spirits business so compelling.

I would also like to thank my parents, Larry and Alice Rothbaum, for their constant support, encouragement, and wisdom and for instilling in me a sense of curiosity and a love of books.

Throughout the writing process, I also heavily relied upon my sister, Rebecca Rothbaum, a fellow writer, for advice. I am indebted to Rebecca for her insights.

References

....

INTRODUCTION

Associated Press. 2007. Bourbon producers expanding plants in Kentucky. February 18.

Bandow, D. 2004. NASCAR nannies. Cato Institute, December 30. Available at www.cato.org/pub_display.php?pub_id=2929.

Clarke, L. 2004. NASCAR to allow hard liquor sponsors. *Washington Post,* November 11. Available at www.washingtonpost.com/wp-dyn/articles/A39819-2004Nov10.html.

Davis, A. 2007. A Beam-ing business. *Courier-Journal* (Louisville, KY), February 13. Available at www.courier-journal.com/apps/pbcs.dll/article?AID=/20070213/NEWS01/702130402/-1/NLETTER01.

Harris, M. 2004. NASCAR lifts ban on liquor ads for cars. Associated Press, November 11. Available at the *Daily Iowan,* www.dailyiowan.com (Iowa City, IA).

Lauro, P. W. 2000. Cocktail hour returns to TV. *New York Times,* December 7. Reprinted by Commercial Alert and available at www.commercialalert.org/news/Archive/2000/12/cocktail-hour-returns-to-tv.

Trexler, P. 2006. Ohioans loading up on more liquor. *Beacon Journal* (Akron, OH), December 9.

CHAPTER 1

Bans on off-premises Sunday sales. Alcohol Policy Information System: A project of the National Institute on Alcohol Abuse and Alcoholism. Available at http://alcoholpolicy.niaaa.nih.gov/SundaySales/.

Clark, N. H. 1997–2007. Prohibition. *Microsoft® Encarta® Online Encyclopedia 2007,* http://encarta.msn.com (accessed June 5, 2006).

Goldberg, J. M. *The American Experience with Alcohol,* 2nd ed.: National Alcohol Beverage Control Association. Available from www.nabca.org (free registration).

Guided Readings: The Jazz Age—The American 1920s. 2002–2006. New York: The Gilder Lehrman Institute of American History. Available at www.gilderlehrman.org/teachers/module17/intro_pop1.html.

Hamill, P. 2007. Raging thirst. Review of *Dry Manhattan: Prohibition in New York City* by M. A. Lerner. *New York Times,* March 11. Available at http://query.nytimes.com/gst/fullpage.html?res=9D0CE0DF1631F932A25750C0A9619C8B63.

Lucas, A. 1995. The philosophy of making beer. *Monticello Reports,* April. Charlottesville, VA: Thomas Jefferson Foundation. Available at www.monticello.org/reports/life/beer.html.

Ohio State University Department of History. 2003–2007. *The Brewing Industry and Prohibition.* Columbus, OH: Ohio State University. Available at http://prohibition.osu.edu/brewing/default.cfm (accessed June 5, 2006).

Prial, F. J. 1984. Wine Talk. *New York Times,* January 25.

Robards, T. 1981. In a price war, real wine bargains. *New York Times,* April 8.

Schorske, S., and A. Heckathorn. 2004. Three tier or free trade? *Vineyard & Winery Management,* March/April. Reprinted by Compliance Service of America and available at www.csa-compliance.com/html/Articles/ThreeTierFreeTrade.html.

Thornton, M. 1991. Alcohol prohibition was a failure. In *NABCA Survey Book,* 2005 ed. The Cato Institute (July 17).

Tomasson, R. E. 1982. Era of change for liquor stores. *New York Times,* December 26.

George Washington: The First Distiller

Pogue, D. J., and E. C. White. 2005. *George Washington's Gristmill at Mount Vernon.* Mount Vernon, VA: The Mount Vernon Ladies' Association.

This Beer's for You?

Associated Press. 2006. Anheuser-Busch may enter liquor market. June 22. Available from MSNBC.com at www.msnbc.msn.com/id/13454851/.

CHAPTER 2

Hansell, J. 2003. Why did my favorite whisky go? *Malt Advocate,* fourth quarter.

Peterson, T. 2001. Absolut Michel Roux. *Business Week,* December 4. Available at www.businessweek.com/bwdaily/dnflash/dec2001/ nf2001124_7329.htm.

Romero, S. 2006. Venezuela's cup runs over, and the Scotch whiskey [sic] flows. *New York Times,* August 20. Reprinted by *Venezuela Real* and available at http://venezuelareal.zoomblog.com/archivo/ 2006/10/06/venezuelas-Cup-Runs-Over-and-the-Scotc.html.

CHAPTER 3

Asimov, E. 2005. "A humble old label ices its rivals," Spirits of the Times. *New York Times,* January 26. Available at http://www. nytimes.com/2005/01/26/dining/26wine.html?ex=126448200 0&en=5913ec796f54a33c&ei=5088&partner=rssnyt.

Clifford, Stephanie. 2005. Q&A: Sidney Frank, Everything in good time (interview with Sidney Frank). *Inc.,* September 2005.

Elliott, S. 2005. Vodka goes beyond plain vanilla. *New York Times,* June 16.

Felten, E. 2006. The emperor's new vodka. *The Wall Street Journal,* January 7. Reprinted by the State of Iowa Alcoholic Beverages Division and available at http://publications.iowa.gov/archive/ 00003306/01/January_13__2006_e-News.doc#Two.

Freedman, A. M. 1981. Rolls-Royces of ice cream. *New York Times,* February 22. Available at http://query.nytimes.com/gst/fullpage. html?sec=health&res=9D06E5D91739F931A15751C0A967948260.

Furlotte, N. 2000. The flavor of vodka. *Cheers,* May. Available at www.beveragenet.net/cheers/2000/0500/0500vod.asp .

Gimbel, B. 2006. Buying by the bottle. *Fortune,* January 30. Available at http://money.cnn.com/magazines/fortune/fortune_archive/2006/02/06/8367972/index.htm.

Hevesi, D. 2006. Rose Mattus, 90, co-creator of Häagen-Dazs ice cream, dies. *New York Times,* December 1. Available at www.nytimes.com/2006/12/01/obituaries/01mattus.html?ex=1322629200&en=8412b912549fbbc3&ei=5090&partner=rssuserland&emc=rss.

Howard, T. 2004. Absolut puts a new premium on vodka. *USA Today,* March 31. Available at www.usatoday.com/money/industries/food/2004-03-30-vodka_x.htm.

Koerner, B. I., 2004. Openers: The goods; Selling the chill factor (and the vodka). *New York Times,* May 16.

Kummer, C. 2004. Flavorless no more. *Atlantic Monthly,* December. Available at www.theatlantic.com/doc/200412/kummer.

Mervine, B. 2005. The art of vodka. *Orlando Business Journal* (FL), December 20. Available at http://orlando.bizjournals.com/orlando/stories/2006/01/02/story6.html.

Niemietz, B. 2006. Bottle service: A brief history. *New York Magazine,* June 26. Available at http://nymag.com/nightlife/features/17308/.

Nims, C. 2002. Flavors of the month: An explosion of flavors is fueling the vodka boom. *Cheers,* May. Available at www.beveragenet.net/cheers/2002/0205/0205vod.asp.

Prial, F. J. 2001. "A favorite wherever glasses are lifted," Wine Talk. *New York Times,* February 7. Available at www.nytimes.com/2001/02/07/living/07WINE.html?ex=1175313600&en=5021fcd271ec1953&ei=5070.

Rendon, J. 2004. "Spending: Want to profit from vodka? Follow that Grey Goose," Sunday Money. *New York Times,* October 31. Reprinted by the State of Iowa Alcoholic Beverages Division and available at http://publications.iowa.gov/archive/00001928/01/ November_5,_2004_e-news.doc#First.

Sidney Frank: The Master Marketer

Brady, D. 2004. The wily fox behind Grey Goose. *BusinessWeek,* September 20. Available at www.businessweek.com/magazine/ content/04_38/b3900094.htm.

Ellis, J. 2004. Jägermeister master donates $20 million for academic building. *Brown Daily Herald* (Providence, RI), September 7. Available from http://media.www.browndailyherald.com/home/.

Fauchald, N. 2005. Wine from a windfall. *Wine Spectator,* May 15. Available at www.winespectator.com/Wine/Archives/Show_ Article/0,1275,5006,00.html.

Miller, M. 2004. "Grey Goose billionaire's second act," Entrepreneurs. *Forbes,* September 10. Available at www.forbes. com/2004/09/10/cz_mm_0910goose.html?rl04.

Martin, D. 2006. Sidney Frank, 86, Dies; Took a German drink and a vodka brand to stylish heights. *New York Times,* January 12.

Stevenson, S. 2005. The cocktail creationist. *New York Magazine,* January 10. Available at http://nymag.com/nymetro/news/ bizfinance/biz/features/10816/.

The Famous Face of High-end Spirits

Miles. J. 2006. Shaken and stirred: Design for drinking. *New York Times,* May 28.

Steinberger, M. 2005. Chateau Elvis: Which celebrities make the best wine? *Slate,* February 16. Available at http://slate.msn.com/Default.aspx?id=2113608.

Spirits Advertising

Minneapolis/St. Paul Business Journal. 2003. Belvedere Vodka takes competitor to court over ad claims. September 9. Available at www.bizjournals.com/twincities/stories/2003/09/08/daily16.html.

Hein, K. 2006. Liquor ads are pervasive, study says. *Brandweek,* December 20. Available at www.adweek.com/aw/national/article_display.jsp?vnu_content_id=1003523836.

Howard, T. 2006. Absolut gets into spirit of name play with new ads. *USA Today,* January 16. Available at www.usatoday.com/money/advertising/2006-01-16-absolut-usat_x.htm.

CHAPTER 4

Conrad III, B. 2006. "Movers and shakers," Collectors. *ForbesLife,* June 19. Available at http://members.forbes.com/fyi/2006/0619/063.html.

DeGroff, D. 2002. *The Craft of the Cocktail.* New York: Clarkson Potter.

De Lollis, B. 2006. Hotel bars morph into stylish multitaskers. *USA Today,* June 1. Available at www.usatoday.com/money/biztravel/2006-07-31-hotel-bars2-usat_x.htm.

Greene, G. 1998. Remembering Joe Baum. *New York Magazine,* October 26. Available at http://nymag.com/nymetro/food/reviews/insatiable/2230/.

Grimes, W. 1998. Joseph Baum, American dining's high stylist, dies at 78. *New York Times,* October 6.

Grimes, W. 2003. "Shaken, stirred or mixed, the Gilded Age lives again," The Critic's Notebook. *New York Times,* March 26. Reprinted and available at www.kingcocktail.com/Times Mar2003.htm.

Hamilton, W. L. 2004. *Shaken and Stirred.* New York: Harper Collins.

Miller, B. 1989. Restaurants. *New York Times,* August 4.

Sell, S. 2006. Raise your glasses to "the year of the cocktail" (interview with Dana Cowin). *USA Today,* January 19. Available at www. usatoday.com/travel/destinations/2006-01-19-cocktails_x.htm.

Visakay, S. 1997. *Vintage Bar Ware Identification & Value Guide.* Paducah, KY: Collector Books.

Wondrich, D. 2006. Great moments in bartending. *Esquire,* June. Available at www.esquire.com/features/ESQ0606BARSrev_107_3.

Dale DeGroff: Master Mixologist

DeGroff. D. 2002. *The Craft of the Cocktail: Everything You Need to Know to Be a Master Bartender, with 500 Recipes.* New York: Clarkson Potter.

Miller. B. 1989. Restaurants. *New York Times,* August 4.

CHAPTER 5

Surowiecki, J. 2006. "Deal sweeteners," The Financial Page. *New Yorker,* November 11. Available at www.newyorker.com/archive/2006/11/27/061127ta_talk_surowiecki.

CHAPTER 6

O'Connor, V. 2005. Yo, ho, ho and a fancy new bottle of "superpremium" rum. *The Wall Street Journal,* December 27.

Salkin, A. 2006. Fame at 70 proof. *New York Times,* October 1. Available at www.nytimes.com/2006/10/01/fashion/01Liquor. html?ex=1317355200&en=3c1b57f4ba2275b7&ei=5088& partner=rssnyt&emc=rss.

Stevenson. S. 2005. The cocktail creationist. *New York Magazine,* January 10. Available at http://nymag.com/nymetro/news/bizfinance/biz/features/10816/.

Cognac: The Spirits of Kings

Berfield, S. 2003. The CEO of hip-hop. *BusinessWeek,* October 27. Available at www.businessweek.com/magazine/content/03_43/b3855001_mz001.htm.

CHAPTER 7

Ball, D., and A. Zimmerman. 2005. A sober Wal-Mart launches drive into tricky area: Liquor. *The Wall Street Journal,* August 17.

Index

....

A

ABK6, 154
Absolut, xii, 28, 44, 46, 48, 51, 73
Absolut Peppar, 51–52
Absolute Vodka, 58–59
Adams Beverage Group, 51
Advertising, 58–61
Advertising Age, 59
Agave, 135–36
Agriculture Department, 97
Agua Luca, 133, 149, 150
Albertsons, 165
"Alcohol Prohibition Was a Failure,"
    11
Alcohol sales, 4–5
Alize, 155
Alvarex-Peters, Annette, 165
Amendoim cask, 147
American Distilling Institute, xv
American Honey, 99
American whiskey, 102
Anchor Distilling, 83
Anchor Steam Beer, 83, 123
Ancient Age, 48
Anderson, James, 6

Anejo tequila, 136, 137, 138–40, 142
"Angel's share," 45
Anheuser-Busch, xi, 15
Applebee's, 92
Apple martini, 54, 67
Aquavit, 162
Archer Daniels Midland, 44
Armadale vodka, 55
Associated Press, xiv, 15
Atomic Age, 71
Auchentoshan, 21
Auction market, 32
Aurora, 77
Australian Yellow Tail wine, 163
Azqueta, Aleco, 43, 50, 51

B

Bacardi, 47, 49, 132, 138, 139
Baccarat decanter, 33
Baccarat, 156
Baileys, 98
Bakelite, 71
Balance and Columbian Repository,
    The, 67–68

Balvenie, 28, 35
Bambu White Rum, 148
Bank Exchange saloon, 69
Bar and Books, 83, 84, 87
Bar Arts program, 88
Baron, Fabien, xii, 138
Barrel, 105, 107–8
Basquiat, Jean-Michel, 28
"Bathtub gin," 11
Baton Rouge Advocate, 48
Baum, Joe, 74, 77–78
Beam, Craig, 113, 114–15
Beam, Parker, 115
Beattie, Scott, 67
Beecher, Rev. Lyman, 5
Beefeater Gin, 132, 162
Beer, 9, 14–15
Beeradvocate.com, 14
Bel Geddes Norman, 70, 82
Beleza Pura Caipirinha, 149, 150
Bell's, 25
Belvedere vodka, 45, 46, 55, 60
Ben & Jerry, 62
Benromach, 33
Bergeron, Victor, 71, 72–73
Berlic, Olie, 149, 151
Bernheim Original Kentucky Straight
    Wheat Whiskey, 105
Beverage Testing Institute, 45
Beveridge, Tito, 13, 52
Bitters, 81
Black Orpheus, 148
Blanco tequila, 134, 136, 137, 140
Blended whiskies, 20, 22, 26, 31–32,
    36–37, 101, 121
Blue agave, 137
Blue Agave Cabo Wabo Tequila, 55
Blue Hawaii, 73
Blue Hen Vodka, 53
Blue laws, 4, 5
Blue Ribbon, 75
Blue Weber agave, 135–36
Bond, James, 43
Booker's bourbon, 104
Bootleggers, 10–11

Bordeaux, x, 141
Bordeaux's Margaux commune, 108
Boston Shaker, 69–70, 90
Bourbon, x, 5, 102–3, 105–6,
    112–18, 121, 123
Boutique spirits, 131–34
Bowman, Joe, 133, 149, 151
Bradshaw, Carrie, 49, 84
Brandweek, 58–59
Brandy, 152, 153
Brandy Alexander, 157
Brandy Library (New York), 22
Branson, Richard, 163
Bravo, xiv
Brewers Association, 14
Brown-Foreman, xiv, 104
Bruichladdich, 33
Buddha's Hand, 53
Buffett, Jimmy, 134
Bundchen, Gisele, 148
Bunnahabhain Distillery, 110
Burgundy, 108
Burj Al Arab hotel, 89
Busch IV, August, 15
Business Week, 47, 153

C

Cachaca, 133, 147, 148–51
Caipirinha, 149
Calabrese, Salvatore, 86
California Gold Rush, 68
Calvin Klein, 138
Camarena, Carlos, 141
Campbell, John W., 86
Campbell Apartment, 84, 86
Canadian Club, 121
Canadian whisky, 102
Cape Code, 54
Carroll, Matt, 140
CasaMagna Marriott, 141
Casino Royale, 43
Cato Institute, 11
Cavalli, Roberto, 46, 56
Celebrity vodka, 55–56

Center on Alcohol Marketing and
Youth (CAMY), xiv, 61
Chablis, 97
Chambord, 98
Champagne, 43, 136, 156, 162
Chanterelle, 143, 144
Charbay, 52
Chardonnay, 97
Charley O's, 76–77
Chassing, Stephanie, 146, 147, 148
Chavez, Hugo, 23
Chiang Monika, 67, 83
Chicago Beverage Testing Institute, 60
Chivas Regal, 20, 22, 31–32, 101
Chocolate, 119
Chopin vodka, 46, 60
Christian Brothers brandy, 105
Christie's, 32
Churchill, Winston, 26
Cigar Aficionado, x
Cipriani family, 75, 78
Civil War, 9, 69
cK One perfume, xii, 138
Clooney, Rosemary, 89
CNN, xiv
Coale, Ansley, 53
Cobbler Shaker, 90
Cocktail, xv–xvi, 65–93, 132, 165–66
cookbooks, 91–92
dinners, 75
menu, 85–87
shaker, 69–70, 81–82
Coffey, Aeneas, 24
Coffey Stills, 24
Cognac, 24, 41–42, 49, 100, 120,
151, 152–57
blends, 154–55
Cognac Ferrand, 156, 157
"Cognac Room," 153–54
Coke, xii, xvii, 85, 132
Cole, Natalie, 75
Cole, Nat King, 75
Coleman, Frank, xiii, 61
Commander's Palace, 75
Compass Box Whisky, 21, 30–31

Computerization, 28
Connick Jr., Harry, 75
Consumption, 13–14
Control states, 13
Cookbooks, 119, 126
Cooley Distillery, 110
Coppola, Francis Ford, 55
Corazon tequila, xii, 47, 139
Corzo tequila, xii, 138
Cosmopolitan, xvi, 54, 67, 84, 87,
145
Costco, 164–65
Courvoisier, 153
Cowin, Dana, 66
Craft of the Cocktail, The, 69, 77–78,
92
Craigellachie Hotel, 36
Crate & Barrel, 90
Creative marketing, 132–33
Cristal champagne, xvi, 46
Crowley, Martin, 137
Crown Royal Whisky, 61
Cruise, Tom, 146
Cruises, 89, 92
Crunk energy drink, 47
Cruty, Stephen, 110–11
Cutty Sark, 33
Cyrus, 67

D

Dagorn, Roger, 143, 144
Daiquiri, 69
Dalgarno, Bob, 109
Dalwhinnie, 23
Danzka, 45
Dash, Damon, 55
Dave's Dinners, 119, 126
Day of the Dead dinner, 141
DeBeers, 59
Def Jam Recordings, 153
DeGroff, Dale, 69, 70, 74–78, 88, 92
DeGroff, Jill, 77
DeJoria, John Paul, 137–38
Delta Air Lines, 88

Depression, 71
Despont, Thierry, 89
Dewar's, 101
Dewar's White Label, 48
Diageo, xi, xiv, xvii, 23, 28, 30, 61,
    99, 133, 146–47, 164
DiCaprio, Leonardo, 146
Diddy, P., 152, 153
Dirty martinis, 84
Distilled Spirits Council of the United
    States (DISCUS), x, xi, xiii, 4, 5,
    8, 20, 26–28, 43, 61, 66, 98, 100,
    105, 125, 138, 145, 152, 156
Dogfish Head, xv, 53
Donations, 132
Don Eduardo, 138
Don Julio, 138, 140
Dorchester hotel, 89
Double Seven, 66–67, 83, 92–93
Dr. No, 43
Dylan, Bob, 55

E

Easy Drinking Whisky Company,
    110–11
Eau de vie, 151, 156
eBay, 79, 81
Edelman Leather, 33
Edrington Group, 107
18th Amendment, 4, 10
El Tesoro, 141
Election Day, 4
Electric coils, 28
Employees Only, 86
Esquire, 67
Evan Williams bourbon, 105
Excalibur Enterprise, 149
"Extra Anejo," 140

F

Fairmont Hotel, 89
Fairmont Miramar Hotel, 33
Fairmont San Jose, 141

Famous Amos Cookies, 133
Ferrand, 156
Fine Oak, 109–10
Fine Oak Macallan, 165
Finlandia, xiv
Fire harvesting, 150–51
Flatiron Lounge, 54, 65–66, 73, 85, 92
Flavored vodka, 56–57
Flavoring, 50–54
Fleming, Ian, 43
Fleur de Sel, 80
Food & Wine, xvi, 31, 66
Food Decade, 82
Food Network, 82, 119
Forbes, 49
Fortune, 50
40/40 Clubs, 153
Forum of the Twelve Caesars, 74, 76
Four Seasons restaurant, 50, 74, 76,
    141
Francis Abecassis, 154
Frank, Eugene, 48
Frank, Sidney, xii, xvii, 45, 47–49,
    59–60, 131, 139
Fraser River Raspberry, 53
Frusen Gladje, 57, 62

G

Garden Variety Vodka Company, 127
Gehry, Frank, 45
Gekkeikan Sake, 48
Genliver, 19
Georgetown University, 61
Georgetown University, xiv, 61
Gershwin tunes, 75
Getz, Stan, 148
Gilberto, Astrud, 148
Gilberto, Joao, 148
Gilder Lehrman Institute of American
    History, 10, 11
Gin, x, 43, 150, 162
"Girl from Ipanema, The," 148
Glaser, John, 30–31
Glaser, Milton, 150

Glass ware, 91
Gledfiddich, xii, xvi, 19, 29, 34–35, 101, 109
Glenfiddich Gran Reserva, 108
Glenlivet, xi, 19, 23, 34, 101, 109
Glenlivet Cellar Collection, 32
Glenlivet Chair, 33
Glenmorangie, 19, 31, 33, 108
Glenrothes, 33
Godiva, 99
Goldstein, Jonathan, 21, 22, 26
Gordon & MacPhail, 27
Gourmet Garage, 80
Gracie Mansion, 77
Grain whisky, 24
Grammy award, 75
Gran Centenario, 138, 140
Grand Central Station, 84
Grand Marnier, 154, 155
Gran Patrón Burdeos, 141
Gran Patrón Platinum, 140–41
Grant, William 35
Grappa, xv
Graves, Michael, 82
Great Depression, 11–12, 70
Green, Martin, 32
Grenadine, 157
Grey Goose Vodka, xi, xii, xvi, xvii, 41–43, 45–50, 59–61, 112, 131–32, 139, 146, 150, 165
Grossich, Mark, 84

H

Haagen-Dazs, 57
Haasarud, Kim, 70, 92
Hagar, Sammy, 55
Hangar One, 53
Hansell, John, 26, 27, 29, 37
Harry's Bar, 75
HBO, 84, 87
Heaven Hill, 105, 113, 114–15, 121–22, 125, 154, 155
Hedonism, 31
Hein, Kenneth, 58–59, 60

Helton, Mike, xiv
Hemingway daiquiri, 86
Hendrix, Jimi, 56
Hendrix Electric, 56
Hennessy, 154
Herb's Aromatic Infused Vodkas, 127
Herbs, 127
"Here's to Beer" campaign, 15
Herman Miller, 33
Highland Park, 21, 28, 31, 107
Hine, 157
Hinky Dink, 72
Holland America line, 89
Home bar, 90–92
Hospitality Holdings, 84
Hotel Bel-Air, 77
How to Mix Drinks or the Bon Vivant's Companion, 69
Howard Johnson, 76
Hpnotiq, 155
Hughes, Bill, 106
Hurricane Katrina, 66
Hyafil, Jerome, 127

I

Ice cubes, 91
Iconoclasts, 132
Inc., 45
Independent bottlers, 27
Indiana Jones, 3
Information Resources, x
"Inquiry into the Effects of Ardent Spirits, An," 8
International Wine and Spirit Record, xi, 14
Internet, 79
Irish whiskey, 100, 102
Iron Chef, 142

J

J&B, 25
Jack Daniel's, xiv, 102
Jagerdudes, 48

Jagerettes, 48
Jagermeister, 45, 48, 131
Jagger, Jade, 89
Jay-Z, 55, 152, 153, 154
Jazz Age, 70
Jekyll & Hyde, 15
Jell-O, xvi
JetBlue, 163
Jim Beam, xii, 99, 113, 116–18,
   121, 123
Jim Beam's Old Overholt, 125
Jim Beam's Small Batch Bourbon
   Collection, 104
Jimadors, 136
John Paul Mitchell Systems, 137
John, Olivia Newton, 55
Johnnie Walker, xiv, 22, 25, 28, 30,
   101, 118
Johnnie Walker Black Label, 24, 25
Johnnie Walker Blue Label, 32–33,
   118–19
Johnnie Walker Gold Label, 118
Johnnie Walker Green Label, 118
Jose Cuervo, 135, 138
Jose Cuervo's Reserva de la Familia,
   139–40
"Joy of Sake," 143
Juices, 84
JW Marriott Starr Pass Resort &
   Spa, 141

K

Kaffir Lemon, 53
Kahlo, Frida, 56
Kahlua, 98
"Kaiser brew," 10
Kass, Larry, 121, 122, 154–55
Katz, Allen, 120
Kendall-Jackson, 82
Kentucky Distillers' Association, 117
Ketel One, 146, 150
Kirkland Signature Vodka, 164–65
Kobrand, 155
Krall, Diana, 89

L

La Fonda del Sol, 76
Lagasse, Emeril, 55
Lagavulin Scottish whisky, 23, 29, 75,
   119
Lalique decanter, xii
Landy Cognac, 157
Landy Cognac's Desir, 154
Laphroaig, 119
Leblon cachaca, 151
LeNell's, 126
Level vodka, 46
Lever Food and Fuel Act, 10
Leyenda, 140
Liberman, 126
Lieberman, Dave, 119, 126
Lil' John, 47
Lime Twisted Gin, 61
Limited edition bottles, 155–56
Limousin oak casks, 140
Liqueurs, 97–127
Liquid Architecture, 70, 92
Liquid Kitchen, 92
Liquor stores, xv
Long Tail Libations, 15
Louis XIII Black Pearl, 156
Louisiana State Museum, 79
Louisiana State University, 48
Lumsden, Bill, 108
Luttman, Steve, 151

M

Macallan, xii, xvi, 29, 32–33, 35, 99,
   101, 107–10, 157, 165
Macallan Amber, 99
Macallan Fine & Rare Collection,
   32–33
Macallan's Cask Strength, 26
MacLean, Gil, 81
MacRae, Caspar, 109
Madeira, 108
Madera, 107
Madison, James, 5

Madonna, 138
Mae de Ouro, 150–51
Magarian, Ryan, 92
Magic Castle, 77
Mai tai, 71, 72–73
Maker's Mark, 8, 100, 103–5, 113, 117–18
Malaga, 108
Malt Advocate Magazine, 26, 31, 33, 36, 125
Manhattans, 66, 69, 120–21, 126
Manifest X.O: Style Fundamentals for the Good Life, 154
Map Room (Chicago), 14
Margarita, 132, 134, 142
"Margaritaville," 134
Marilyn Wines, 55
Marinis, 66
Marriott, 88
Marshall, James W., 68
Martini, 69, 71, 132
Master's Collection, 105
Match Bar, 86–87
Mathilde Raspberry, 157
Mattus, Reuben, 57, 62
Maytag, Fritz, 83, 123–24
McMahon, Ed, 55, 56
McTear's, 32
Medical community, 6, 8–9
Meyer, Danny, 119
Mezcal, 136
Microdistilleries, xv
Midori melon liqueur, 99
Millar, Ian, 29
Millenium Import company, 60
Miller, Bryan, 77
Milwaukee Art Museum, 79
Mining towns, 68–69
Mixed whiskeys, 119
Mixologists, 66–67, 80–81
Mixto, 136
Moet Hennessy, 146
Mojito, 145, 149
Mondavi, Robert, 82
Monroe, Marilyn, 55

Moonshine, 11
Morimoto, 142
Morris, Chris, 104–5, 113
Moss, Kate, 89
Mr. & Mrs. T, 80
MTV, 148
Muddling, 91
Murray, Douglas MacLean, 28, 118–19
Museum of the American Cocktail, 66, 78

N

Napoleon, 152
NASCAR teams, xiv
National Alcoholic Beverage Control Association (NABCA), 5, 8–10, 13
National Conference of State Liquor Administrators, 15
National Prohibition Act, 10
Nelson, Willie, 55
New York Magazine, 50
New York Nightlife Association, 50, 92
New York Post, 132
New York Times, 5, 23, 48, 77, 87–88, 124
Nightclub bottle service, 49–50, 92–93
Nike, 59
Nintendo, 144
"Noble Experiment," 12
Noe, Booker, 104, 116
Noe, Fred, 104, 105, 112–14, 116–18
Norman, Greg, 55
Notting Hill, 87

O

Oban, 29
Ohio State University, 9
Old-fashioned, 120
Old Potrero Single Malt Hotaling's Whiskey, 124

Old Potrero Single Malt Whiskey, 124
Old Potrero Straight Rye Whiskey, 124
Old Whiskey Bourbon, 55
101 Martinis, 70, 92
Opus One, 82
Oronoco, 146, 147
Owens, Bill, xv

P

Pama, 98
Park Avenue Liquor Shop, 21–22, 26
Parker, Robert, 55, 83
Parker, Sarah Jessica, 84
Partida Tequila, 133, 134, 138
Party sponsorships, 131–32
Patrón, xi, 99, 137–38, 140–41, 148
Pearce, Chris, 143
Peat Monster, 31
Pegu Club, 54, 66, 73, 85
People, 146
Pepsi, 44
Pepsico, 44
Pernod Ricard, 132, 138–39
Phat Farm, 153
Phillips, Dean, 98, 111–12
Philips, 79
Phillips Distilling Company, 98, 111
Phillips Union, 111, 112
Phylloxera virus, 24
Pickerell, Dave, 103, 113, 117–19
Pimm's cup, 86
Pineau des Charentes, 154–55
Pokemon, 144
Port, 24, 107–8
Pottery Barn, 90
Pratt & Whitney, 48
Pravda Vodka, 45–46, 60
Premium product, 162
Premium spirits, xi–xii
Presley, Elvis, 73
Prial, Frank J., 5
Pricing, 163
Prince Andrew, 8

Private Label Manufacturers
    Association, 165
Prohibition, xiii–xv, xvii, 3–6,
    8–13,15–16, 70, 84, 92, 102, 120
Promenade Bar, 78
Pug! Muddler, 91
Pursuits, 88

Q

Quaich Bar, 36
Queen Elizabeth, 152
Quixote, Don, 103

R

Rabin, David, 50, 92
Rainbow Room, 74, 75, 78
Rare bottlings, 32
RCA, 47
Red Breast, 100
Red Hook Rye, 126
Reiner, Julie, 54, 73, 83, 84, 92
Remy Dragon, 157
"Remy Lounge," 154
Remy Martin, 155, 157
Remy Martin Louis XIII, 156
Remy Red, 155
Renaissance, 88
Reposado tequila, 136, 137, 142
Restaurant Associates, 77
Restoration Hardware, 82
Retail sales, 3–4
Rhymes, Busta, 152, 153
Ribeiro, Roberto, 147
Ribeiro, Vicente Bastos, 147
Rich Spicy One, 110
Riedel, xv
Rieslings, 97
Rittenhouse Rye, 125
Roaring Twenties, 11
Robertson, David, 110
Roc-A-Fella Records, 55
Roosevelt, Franklin Delano, 12

Rosa Mexicano, 141
Rosen, Adam, 56, 57
Rosenstiel, Louise "Skippy," 47, 48
Rothschild, Baron Philippe de, 82
Roux, Michel, 28
Rum, x, xii, 5, 43, 144–48
Rumrunners, 10–11
Rupf, Jorg, 53
Rush, Dr. Benjamin, 8–9
Russell, Eddie, 8, 99, 107, 113, 115–16
Russell, Jimmy, 99, 106–7, 113, 116, 161–62
Russell's Reserve, 106
Russian Vodka Room, 56
Rye whiskey, ix–x, 5, 102, 119, 120–26

S

S&P 500 Index, xii
Sake, 142–44
Saloons, 9
Salvatore at Fifty, 86
Samson, Savanna, 55
Samuels family, 118
Samuels Jr., Bill, 8, 100, 103–4
Samuels Sr., Bill, 100
Samuels, T. W., 100
Sarnoff, David, 47
Sarnoff, Edward, 47
Saturday Night Live, 61
Saunders, Audrey, 66
Sauvignon blanc, 97
Sazerac, 120
Scapa, 33
Schenley Distilleries, 47–48
Scotch whisky, xiii, 19–20, 123
Scotch Whisky Association, xiii, 19–20, 31
Scott, Colin, 20, 31
Scott, Ridley, 35
Scottish Exchequer, 23
Scottish single malt whisky, 19

Scottish whisky, 165
Scottish Whisky Trail, 34–36
Screaming Eagle, 82–83
Screwdriver, 54
Seagram, 61
Senor Pico, 72
Sex, 138
Sex and the City, xv, 49, 84
Shaker, 70–71, 81–82
Shakers tour, 79
Shanken, Marvin, x
Shansby, Gary, 133, 134, 138
Sherry, 24
Sherry casks, 109
Sherry Oak, 110
Sidney Frank Importing, 48
Simmons, Russell, 153
Singapore slings, 66
Single malt whisky, 19–23, 26–27, 29, 33, 36–37, 101, 104, 118–19, 137, 140, 141
Sky View Bar, 89
Skyy Vodka, 54, 163–64
Slow Food USA, 120, 124
Smirnoff, xiv, 43, 44, 61
Smith, George, 23–24
Smokey Peaty One, 110, 111
Smooth Sweeter One, 110, 111
Smothers, Tonya LeNell, 126
Snoop Dogg, 56, 146, 148
Soju, 149
Sour apple martinis, xvi
South Pacific, 73
Southern Wine & Spirits of New York, 120
Southern Wine and Spirits of America, 12
Specialty malters, 28
Speyside Cooperage, 35–36
Spices, 127
Spice Tree, 31
Spices, 127
Spirits consumption, x–xi
"Spirits Desk," 132

Spirits of the Times," 124
Sprite, 157
Square One, 53
Starbucks, 97, 99
Starr African Rum, xii, 145–46
State-run stores, 13
StateWays, 139
Statue of Liberty, 59
Sting, 55
Stirrings, 80–81
Stolichanaya (Stoli), 44, 46, 56, 132
Stoli Elit, 46
Stolichanaya Gold, 46
Stone fruit spirits, xv
Stowe, Harriet Beecher, 5
Sundance Channel, 132
Sunday, alcohol purchase on, xv
Suntory International, 99
Supreme Court, 13
Sur La Table, 80
Sutter's Mill, 68
Sweet Ginger Fizz, 111
Swingers, 75, 78

T

T.G.I. Friday's, 80
Tabla, 119
Talisker, 23, 29
Tanqueray No. Ten, 162
Tanqueray Rangpur Gin, 133
Tanqueray Ten, xvii
Target, 82
Tastings, xv, 5
10 Cane Rum, 146–47, 148
Tennessee whiskey, 105
Tequila, x, 132, 134–42, 150
Tequila Don Julio, xi
Tequila Regulatory Council, 140
Terra Chips, 133
Tezon, 139
Thin Man, The, 84
Thomas, Jerry, 69
Thornton, Mark, 11
Three-tier system, 12–13, 15–16

Tiki drink, 71, 73
Times Square, 76
Tito's Handmade Vodka, 13, 52
Tom Collins, 91
Torme, Mel, 89
Trader Joe's, 165
"Trader Vic," 71, 72–73, 88
Trailer Happiness, 73, 87
Tribute, 107
Tron, 62
Tropicalia, 148
Trump, Donald, 56
Tudor, Frederic, 68
21 Club, 3
21st Amendment, 3, 4, 13
Two Buck Chuck, 165

U

Unforgettable, 75
United, 88
University of Kentucky, 115
USA Network, xiv
USA Today, 66
US Weekly, 132, 146

V

Valentine's Day Massacre, 11
Van Gogh vodka, 51
Variety Arts Club, 77
Vaughn, Vince, 78
Vesper, 43
Veuve Clicquot, 150
Vinexpo conference, xi, 14, 152
Vintage Bar Ware, 69 79
Vintage spirits, 156–57
Virgin Atlantic, 163
Virgin Drinks, 163
Virgin Vodka, 163
Visakay, Stephen, 69, 70, 79, 82
Vodka, xi–xii, 28, 37, 41–62, 99,
  111–12, 121, 123, 127, 132–34,
  139, 142, 144, 146, 149–50,
  163–64

Vogue, xii
Von Ertfelda, Matthew, 88

W

Wall Street, xiii
Wall Street Journal, The, 45, 49, 88,
 264
Wal-Mart, 15–16, 164
Warhol, Andy, 28, 58
Washington, George, ix, 5, 6–7, 120
West Side, 86
West Side Story, 76
When Harry Met Sally, 75
Whiskey, x, 6–7
Whisky, xii, 19–37, 43, 99–102,
 110–12, 120, 137
WhiskyFest, 36, 125
Whisky Magazine, 31
White rum, 144–45, 147–48
Whole Foods Market, 80, 82, 165
Wild Turkey, xvii, 8, 99, 106–7, 113,
 115–16, 132, 161–62
Wild Turkey Wild Breed, 104
William Grant & Sons, 29
Williams, Pharrell, 148

Williams-Sonoma, 80
Windows on the World, 74
Wine, 82–83, 107, 163
Wine casks, 107–8
Wine Spectator, x
Wondrich, David, 67–70, 75
Woodford Reserve, 104–5, 113
World Beverage Championships
 (2004), 45–46
World Sake Imports, 143
World Spirits Competition, 60, 125
World War I, 26, 156
World War II, 26, 70, 71, 121, 157
Wray & Nephew Jamaican rum, 71
Wright, Russell, 70, 79, 82
Wyborowa, 45

X–Z

XO Café, 99
Yamazaki whisky, 99
Year of the Lady," 156
Zarnow, Jeffrey, 145–46
Zen Green Tea Liqueur, 99